UPSIDE

A GUIDE TO ACHIEVING YOUR UNIQUE POTENTIAL IN LIFE

What lies behind you and what lies in front of you pales in comparison to what lies within you.

— RALPH WALDO EMERSON

JOHN GREGORY VINCENT

ISBN-10: 0615773443
ISBN-13: 9780615773445

Table of Contents

Preface

To know even one life has breathed easier
because you have lived. This is to have succeeded.
— Ralph Waldo Emerson

I can still remember being a little boy growing up on Long Island in Greenlawn, New York, and having dreams of becoming a professional baseball player. I would spend hours in our basement, glove in hand, and with the tennis ball serving as the baseball. In my mind, I was the pitcher, I was the batter, and I was all the fielders. I would play an entire ball game throwing that tennis ball against the wall. I remember it today as clearly as if I were in that basement. But that was forty years ago.

What about you? What dreams did you have when you were a child? Have you ever thought about what happened to them? In my case, it became evident at some point that I did not have the talent to play at a major league level, and so that dream faded. But it was replaced with a new one, and then another , and another. The question is, did I "quit" on my baseball dream because I really did not have the talent, or was I simply influenced by my environment, specifically by events and by people who believed I did not have that potential?

I started to write a business book four years ago, and it went nowhere. Only after I had gotten to a place in my personal journey where I was embracing a one-life approach to living, and sharing it with people in workshops and speeches, did I realize the power this message has on people. I threw away four years of drivel and replaced it with this, written in three months, beginning to end. Furthermore, I began to think about all the advice I had received—career advice and personal advice—and came to the conclusion they were one and the same. Most of the advice I got, besides from my parents, was bad. But the good advice was good for both my career *and* my personal life. At some point all of this hit me, like a ton of bricks, the reason, "good" is good everywhere or bad is bad everywhere is because I have only *one life*.

One reality in life is that, almost from birth, we are bombarded with negative talk and events that we misinterpret as signs of our limitations, as we are made to understand them. Particularly troubling is that much of the negativity comes from those closest to us. Of course, these people who hold us dear to their hearts, don't want to see us hurt or disappointed. So we're fed with a steady diet of "be realistic," "stop kidding yourself," "stop dreaming and start thinking about reality." I was very fortunate; I didn't hear too many directives from my parents. I'm sure they found it strange that their son spent hours and hours in that basement playing the precursor to an online fantasy baseball league, but neither of them ever told me to stop. Neither ever said that I was being silly or that I was wasting my time.

My parents always encouraged me to work hard in school and to work hard in life. Being the quintessential traditionalists, they instilled in me the possibilities that come with hard work, and that work ethic ran parallel with the critical importance of education. I recall my father sitting me down and telling me that without a formal education past the high school level, I would be burdened with challenges and obstacles that would not exist with at least a bachelor's degree. It was great advice, considering a little-known fact about unemployment. We hear it daily: 8 percent unemployment, 9 percent, *yikes*! But unemployment for college graduates with at least an undergraduate degree has been below 5 percent for a long time.

Unemployment numbers are driven by those with no college education, with the rate hovering around 20 percent at the writing of this book. Unlike my older brother and sisters, who all achieved greatness in traditional academic pursuits, I took a path to knowledge and the application of knowledge that was untraditional. I'm fairly certain I never read an entire book from beginning to end until I was in my mid-thirties. Yes, I graduated from high school, and yes, I completed a little bit more than two years of college at State University of New York, Maritime College, in Bronx, New York. I was a 4.0 partygoer and a 1.4 academic. I incorrectly assumed that State University of New York would add those two numbers together, divide by two, and give me a passing grade of 2.7.

Although I certainly didn't embrace traditional schooling shortly after my entrance into the US Navy's submarine force in 1983, I absolutely embraced learning and, more specifically, applying what I learned. In fact, without question, I became a fanatic, specifically in the area of navigation. I wanted to learn and then apply every aspect of navigation in the submarine world.

This was when I first began to understand the power of seeing an outcome—in this case, becoming the most knowledgeable and respected submarine navigator in the Atlantic Fleet, and then putting a plan together and seeing it through. Here's a point of clarification for my fellow navy veterans: I'm a PROUD retired ENLISTED man. I retired in 2003 as a command master chief who spent nearly 75 percent of his twenty-year career on submarines. SUBMARINES FOREVER, folks!

I'm using the word *navigator* here for those of you without knowledge of the United States Navy. I actually was a quartermaster, which is an enlisted service rating for those specializing in navigation.

Now back to the previously started preface. Despite my struggles with alcohol and some other challenges, I had an extremely successful career in the navy, which I talk about in more detail a bit later. As is the case with all my personal stories, the point is not to share how wonderful I am, nor how flawed I am, but to share how human I am, just like you, and completely different than you, at the same time. The real take away from the stories, and indeed from the book is the fact that achieving *your* unique potential can be done, even if you are carrying a heavy life load.

In a later career, I used much of what is discussed in this small book to become one of if not the most junior sales managers ever in a major media company. After that came a small business startup from *nothing* that has grown beyond *any* dreams, or business plans, in less than five years, and it continues to grow exponentially. The Genesis Group LLC, www.gconsultinggrp.com (first of a few shameless plugs), now pays me a very comfortable salary, but much more importantly it helps others maximize *themselves*, and that is cool. Along the way I also fully grasped the one-life concept, which is another critical theme throughout this book, and my personal affairs began to come together as they never had before. I went through an unpleasant divorce (as if there is such a thing as a pleasant one), walked away with a pile of debt and not much else. Starting over without much of anything other than great health and a belief in seeing opportunities rather than problems and then taking action, can take you to a wonderful place. I am now blessed with the most amazing partner anyone could ever have. She has helped me reach a level of fully living life that went beyond even my optimism. This stuff works!

So how did all this come to be? Well, it did not really start all that well when I was a young man, but it evolved, so to speak. I was a college throw out (dropouts sort of leave on their own; I was asked to go away), so I didn't feel I was particularly brilliant, and I certainly wasn't connected to anyone of importance. Despite having a significant drinking problem and some other mental issues as well, I also was on my way to a really successful career in the navy, so I was on to something. I started taking notes of the things I did differently from those around me. I still have some of those notes, long since converted into electronic form.

I did three things consistently that most of the people around me did not do. First and foremost, I ignored the bad advice of my peers, my superiors, and my friends. These people had the best of intentions as they tried to manage my expectations by telling me all the things I could not do instead of encouraging me to go after what was technically possible. I ignored them, having the best of intentions as well. Just because many people decide to settle for a certain station doesn't mean you have to do the same. This doesn't mean anyone is a bad person or lazy person, but it does reiterate a very simple truth: *nobody else is you; nobody can decide for you except you.*

The second thing I did differently from most people is that my first thought was always about what the outcome would look like, feel like, smell like, and taste like. The third thing that separated me was that once I had this vision, once I had this thought, I would put together specific steps that later became known to me as goals—the steps to get to that vision. These three things led a troubled individual and transformed him into someone who was on his way to reaching his full potential in one area of his life.

I used the word *troubled* in the last paragraph; so now is a good time to just lay my cards on the table for you. I had been struggling mightily with many demons that challenged me to my very core most of my adult life. For my entire military career, and for many years before I entered the navy, I was an active alcoholic. I never drank at sea, but when I was in port, I was almost always drunk by sunset. I have been a sober, grateful, recovering alcoholic for ten years now, and without question it is where my embracing of "one life" and achieving my unique potential in life began.

Additionally, I knew from a very young age that my mind didn't work like other people's minds. I constantly had dozens, if not hundreds, of thoughts bouncing around in my head at the same time. I had a great deal of trouble reading anything from page 1 to 2 to 3. I much preferred to start in the middle of the book and read a few pages in one direction and then skip someplace else and read a few more pages. I wrote this off to being eccentric.

I also was acutely aware that I had a vicious temper that was often offset by bouts of deep depression. Again, I was aware that my wild swings in emotion were not shared by the majority of people. I knew this, but once again wrote it off as being somewhat eccentric and just kept pushing to reach *my* unique potential in life. I won't bog you down with letters and disorders and such. I will simply tell you that there is a reason I mention my amazing psychiatrist in the acknowledgments section of this book. 'Nuff said.

I am not sharing these deeply personal facts with you to depress you before you even get into the substance of this book. I share them for the sole purpose of telling you that, regardless of the hand we're dealt and regardless of the depths we have gone to in our life, we all have a massive upside. By "upside" I mean the *true* limits of what we can achieve in our life. Not in terms of wealth or other "stuff," but in terms of peace of mind and happiness, true joy, if you will. Almost all of us have a glass ceiling we have allowed to be put in place, and it is keeping us from reaching our full and unique potential. For whatever reason, I never believed there was a glass ceiling in my areas of potential. Not until I got sober did I begin to include all parts of life into my potential. (Before that, it was always career potential, and being a mess in all other areas was a given.) This *unwillingness to accept any form of glass ceiling* helped me in my journey toward success.

You'll notice throughout this book quotes from Ralph Waldo Emerson. Heck, there is even one on the cover! I began my personal journey of discovering my unique potential at the end of 2002. That's the year I began living, for the first time, a sober life. Somewhere along the line since, I discovered the writings of Ralph Waldo Emerson. He was born in 1803, lost his father at the age of eight, and was raised by his mother, Mary Moody, in a state of poverty. He lost his first wife to tuberculosis, the disease he was crippled with for most of his life.

Emerson's first book, *Nature*, was published in 1836. After twelve years, the first five hundred copies had not yet sold out. His second work, *American Scholar*, was delivered in an address to the Phi Beta Kappa society at Harvard College in 1837; this became very popular and, when printed, sold very well. He published more essays in 1841 and was a prolific writer for the rest of his life. He lived most of his years in Concord, Massachusetts, and died in April of 1882 at seventy-nine.

I've read a wide variety of books from a wide variety of authors; yet no writings have struck me or spoken to me as much as the words of Ralph Waldo Emerson. You'll see some of these quotes throughout this book. I want to share three of my favorites with you before you move on to the introduction.

"Do not go where the path may lead; go instead where there is no path and leave a trail."

"For every minute you remain angry, you give up sixty seconds of peace of mind."

"Always do what you are afraid to do."

These three quotations sum up a great deal of this book.

Here is yet another opening thought for you. Knowledge in and of itself is not power. Only when knowledge is applied does it become power. I implore you to read, learn, and apply the simple methodology laid out in this book. Watch as it leads you to a happier, more fulfilling life for you and for those you choose to share it with. (Share your life, that is; I hope everybody buys his or her own copy of the book.)

Introduction

My copy editor says the introduction is where you tell people why you wrote the book, so here goes.

What started out in the late 1980s as simply not letting others decide what my potential was, followed by envisioning the outcome, and then the last step of putting a plan together and executing it, has been modified several times throughout the years. Specifically, I realized that I have a passion for achieving outcomes that started as a vision and turned into a specific result. For a long time, I thought I was just a passionate guy. With the wisdom that comes with age, I began to realize that there were many areas I didn't have passion for, and in those areas, I didn't achieve high levels of success.

This was when it began to occur to me that, like most people, I'm passionate about things I'm good at. And I came to understand fully how important operating in areas of talent is to success. Most of us enjoy doing things we are good at; we enjoy work we have talent in. Once I added this to the methodology, I further refined my quest to help people reach their full and unique potential. *Embracing that all of these powerful, effective tools built for careers completely apply to all areas of life was the final and most significant revision of my thinking.*

There is a billion-dollar self-improvement industry telling you that you can achieve anything you want in life if you believe and try. I really wish I believed that, but I simply don't. What I believe is that once you focus clearly on the outcomes you want and then put together a well-thought-out, highly focused plan to get to those outcomes, you can achieve anything, as long as it's in an area that you have talent in. This is not to say that you can't have a good life doing things in areas outside your talent, but you will never reach your full and unique potential that way. You will also expend a great deal of energy to just keep up and that is no way to live my friend. TALENT is the "unique" in your unique potential. Yes, talent applies to relationships as well as careers, being a parent as well as starting a business, and on and on it goes.

So I wrote this book with the hope that you carry it with you and use it as a reference. This is a simple, practical how-to guide to reaching your full and unique potential in life. If you read it and don't use the information within, it is a waste of whatever you have paid for it. But if you grab one or two things and apply them, I promise you, you will see a difference in how you feel, in what you achieve, and in how you feel about what you achieve.

Additionally, I wrote to share what I have learned through studying, observing, researching, and applying tools, tips, and techniques that all lead me to a more satisfying life, in the hopes it does the same for all who take the time to read it and apply the parts that speak to you. Again, not every page, or perhaps, even every chapter will speak to you but within these pages lies a nugget that, if applied, can propel you into a new orbit, this I promise you. If you looked for this book in Barnes & Noble, it was likely in the self-improvement section. That's one of the largest sections, I suspect, because almost all of us are at least interested in the idea of being a bit "better" in some way. Google "self-improvement" and you get more than eighty *pages* of results. The term "self-improvement" is searched more than seventy-five thousand times a *month*. I didn't want to write just another self-improvement book, mostly because I don't believe *any* book can improve you; only YOU can improve you. This book absolutely can lead to improvement in your life, but not because of this book, because you take action on some of the things you read, because self-improvement comes from you.

I also wanted to write this book to fundamentally disagree with a widely held premise. I completely disagree that one person can motivate another person. A motivational speaker? Fugetaboutit! (Hey, I did go to college in the Bronx before heading south.) Any person can learn, and this book will teach you or reteach you many things. A person also can be inspired by what he or she reads or sees or hears. It is the person that transforms that knowledge and uses that inspiration to create change in his or her life. You are your change agent. One person can inspire another, and that inspiration can lead to motivation, but motivation is internal to each of us—nothing external can cause it.

So am I talking about self-improvement? No. I hope you find things in this book that inspire you to light the spark of *self-empowerment*. Self-empowerment is the fuel that leads to improvement and success. So get inspired, and let that inspiration fuel change in your life so you achieve *your* unique potential in life.

Not all parts or chapters of this book apply to all people. In fact, one of the formative principles of this book is the fact that we are completely different and unique. So if you dedicate an hour or so to dig through this little book, you will find pure gold in some chapters and lead balloons in others. My hope is that when you find a nugget, you do something with it. The thought of helping another person find *the total them, wow that is great stuff!*

A bit more about how to get the most out of this book you have in your hands. Another formative principle of this book is the belief that knowledge is not power; knowledge *applied* is power. One person may read this book and dog-ear dozens of pages, highlight hundreds of words, but not apply them to his life. Another person may read it and find two sentences that strikes her core in a very fundamental way—even if she finds most of the rest of the book either only mildly entertaining or not applicable. She takes immediate action on those two sentences, practices, applies them and practices some more. The first person may profess to have learned a lot, but it is the second person who has changed, for the better and forever.

I assess, speak, train, consult, and coach for a living, and I'm really good at it (another shameless plug). That being said inevitably what people really want to talk to me about when they get me off to the side is how I've overcome challenges to reach some level of success. Without exception, people like people with what I call scars. A scar is what is left when the wound heals. Scars are sometimes visible and sometimes not visible. Without question, people are most interested in learning from someone they can relate to, and every real person relates best to people that have scars, because we all have them, it is part of what makes you, you.

This book is different for one powerful reason: no two people are the same. That's why its subtitle speaks of your *unique* potential. Many factors go into making you who you are: your upbringing, your culture, your personality, your life experiences, your knowledge, your scars and baggage, and your experience; I will refer to these collectively as your *life skills*. You also have talents. And there are even more factors, such as the generation you were born into, your religious beliefs, your ethnicity, and on and on. There are hundreds of thousands of people that share one of these traits with you—perhaps even millions—but nobody shares them all. All these different "ingredients" make us who we are.

OK, many self-improvement books acknowledge that we are all completely different. Yet some are written for people interested in step-by-step procedures. Others are for people who just want the view from thirty thousand feet. Some of us learn kinesthetically by practicing and playing with the tools and concepts presented. If I thought I could write this book in a hundred forms I would, but the critical factor for me was to write something in less than two hundred pages that would fit in your backpack, briefcase, or your purse so you could, and would, actually use it.

What I am left with is this: I encourage you to apply what you read in these pages in your unique way. You might read this electronically. You might be reading this in traditional book form and taking notes in a notebook, or you might take notes in the book itself. You might not take any notes at all, choosing to skip around and grab a nugget here or there. One-size-fits-all fits nobody. I hope this book opens up your mind to look deeper at yourself and to realize that what makes you unique is what allows you to achieve your full potential.

We often look at being different as a problem, but your difference is far and away your best attribute. The rare individuals that are completely comfortable in their own skin have peace of mind and peace of spirit twenty-four hours a day, seven days a week. I am still on my journey to being completely comfortable in my skin, but I can tell you that, during the past ten years, I've gotten closer to it—closer to myself and who I really am. The results have been unbelievably powerful. I hope this book is a gift to you and those you share it with.

Ackowledgements

Theophilo Vincent
1920 – 2013
Darn Dad, that was the best jelly donut ever!

Before this book went to final editing and publishing, I wrote this section. It wasn't that I was struggling to write an acknowledgments section; it just made sense that this project would be done before certain people or certain ideas emerged. I started to write a business book titled *The Cure for the Common Workplace* more than three years before writing this one. I struggled writing that book, and I'm not sure why. It just didn't feel right. Two hundred and forty pages into it, I deleted the entire manuscript. After a few years of doing nothing with respect to writing a book, I sat down and wrote *Upside*.

I bare my soul in this book, with the purpose being to provide real examples that hopefully hit home and lead you to be inspired to reach higher. More importantly my purpose is to share the beautiful place that I am in now. My hope is that there are things in this book that will touch you in a way that causes you to take action. Nothing would make me happier than if one little nugget turned into personal action that leads to a happier, healthier, more peaceful life for someone who reads these pages. Since that is my hope, my acknowledgments are limited to the people that have most profoundly led me to the wonderful place I am in today.

Deb, this book, along with a long list of other things, likely never would have happened if not for your love and support. Grateful is an understatement for the fact that God allowed me to find perhaps the only person on this earth that takes me at face value, accepts me warts and all, and loves me unconditionally (you too Mom and Dad). When I look at those beautiful eyes and see compassion and pride when you look at me, the way it makes me feel defies words. *You* are the love of my life and have touched me and helped me more in our time together than most people do in seventy or eighty years. I love you.

Mom and Dad, the first story in this book is about you two. I have a full grasp on how I was raised by you, and I could dissect bits and pieces that were less than perfect. But the fact is that, through all my trials, all my tribulations, and all the angst, pain, and worry I know I caused you, you never wavered in your encouragement, your support, and your love. It took a lot of years for me to understand how rare your love for me is. I have never been judged or criticized by either of you, but you always shared advice. I will appreciate all of what you have done for the rest of my life. I love both of you.

Captain Brad McDonald, I was too cocky and frankly too drunk to tell you when I first met you that you're the first person and remain the only person I've ever been in awe of. You are the most exceptional leader I've had the privilege of being around. Far more important than that, you genuinely care about those you served with. No matter how many years have passed, I'm pretty sure you've never said no to requests from your shipmates. There are hundreds and hundreds of people I've met that say, "Let me know if there's anything you need." You're far and away the best example of someone who actually does it. Friend for life, thank you for being a positive example for me when I sorely needed one.

Doc A. G., when we first met, I was ready to dismiss you, as I had done to so many before you. Your ability to listen, to advise, and to help me understand my brain while talking more about stereo equipment, decent movies, and good places to eat has always amazed me. You helped me face issues I likely never would have without the trust and support I felt from you. Thank you. You have, without question, helped me get closer to achieving my unique potential, and the peace and happiness that always come with it.

Robyn S., your sudden and shocking death caused me to examine myself and my life like no other single event ever has, or ever will. Nobody knows better than you the struggles I had in so many different areas during the years we knew each other. For a time I wished mightily that we had left each other's worlds on better terms, but now I embrace, understand, and believe that it is what it is. ☺

Perry and Taylor, I'm not so sure I would've been nominated and I am completely sure I never would've won Father of the Year, but as I get older and as I talk to my adult children, I realize I had a massive impact on you. It seems that impact was mostly good. I also know I did my best, and according to "The *Four Agreements*" (it's in the book, keep reading, please), that is the goal. Additionally another powerful piece of this life puzzle is the effect you've had on me. It has been profound and positive, and it has kept me moving when I wanted to quit. There are things I've written in this book that were inspired by the upside I see in both of you. I love you.

My beloved submarine force, you are the gift that keeps giving. You gave me purpose and meaning when I was struggling for both. You gave me deep connections to people that I will cherish forever. You taught me more about people and how they "work" than a thousand books and a hundred years of study. Today is the best day of my life, and now is the best time of my life, but my years on submarines will always be a close second.

What Makes You Unique
and Why It Matters

*To be yourself in a world that is constantly trying to make you
something else is the greatest accomplishment.*
–Ralph Waldo Emerson

I can remember taking my two children to the local county fair in
South Carolina. My son, Perry, and my daughter, Taylor, ages twelve and
ten at the time, were reared largely by their mother due to the extreme
amount of time I spent on sea duty. They had the same parents, the same
environment, the same structure, and yet they were very different. Perry,
much like his dad, was not a big fan of any carnival ride. He would look
at the rust running down the side of the ride and the interesting-looking
ticket takers and opt out of almost every ride.

But Taylor couldn't get enough of *every* ride. To her, the scarier it looked
and the scarier the person taking the tickets looked, the more interested
she was. It's fascinating to see two human beings raised identically from
the same gene pool turn out so completely different. So the answer to the

question posed in the title of this chapter is that everything about every one of you is what makes you unique.

You might wonder what this chapter has to do with achieving your potential. The answer to that question is: just about *everything*. We can go to school and get a bachelor's degree. We can continue and get a master's degree. And some of us will go even further and get a PhD. Some will get an associate's degree. Of course, the largest group is those that don't get a degree past high school. Some people get technical certifications. Some go into the military. Some become firefighters or police officers. Some become musicians, with or without formal training. A precious few make a living in athletics.

Thousands, if not millions, are in more than one of these categories. Thousands, if not millions, share the same title. The reality is that they all have more than one variable, or factor; that is not unique. At the end of the day, what really makes you special is you, not those things we have in common with all those other people, but the completely unique combination of things that make you, you.

I'm starting here with education and vocation but I could have opened up with life experience, or spiritual beliefs, or generational differences, or personalities, the point is we are *all* unique. I also chose education as the first characteristic because, unlike gender, age, race, talent, and so on, education is an acquired uniqueness.

Your level of education is but one tiny thing that makes you unique. Even if you have bachelor's degrees, there are hundreds of different bachelor's degrees out there and a butt ton (navy technical term) of accredited schools that have their own spin, even on the same degree. So you are unique even if you have the common degree with a common concentration. And even if you graduated from the same school after studying the same curriculum as others, what you drew from that will be different from what others drew.

Again, I've started with academics, but there are more factors that go into making you unique than can be captured in two hundred pages of a book. Your race, your upbringing, your parents' beliefs or lack of them, your lack of progress, your value system, your culture, your unique personality, on and on—all affect who you are. We all have different life experiences, work experiences, and levels and types of knowledge. *Your most powerful asset out of all of the things that make you unique is your talent.*

I've heard many great speakers on leadership use the words *skill* and *talent* interchangeably. Typically experience is what we place the premium on if we are hiring someone. If we are seeking to be hired, we tend to highlight our experience, or what some people call skill. Here is my cut on the differences between experience, skill, and talent: Experience, be it life experience or work experience, are the things we physically and mentally go through that become part of our conscious and eventually subconscious minds. Few individuals can process more than five or six simultaneous thoughts in their conscious mind. Most of us start breaking down after two or three. But our subconscious mind is still the fastest supercomputer in the world, capable of processing millions of bits of data a second. Our experience winds up being filed away in our subconscious to be drawn on as needed during day-to-day life.

Sometimes *knowledge* and *experience* are used interchangeably, but they are not the same. Unlike experience, knowledge is not necessarily associated with activity. We can learn things and retain or not retain them. There is an application aspect to experience that doesn't necessarily exist with knowledge. You've likely heard that knowledge is power. There is a massive assumption in that statement that shouldn't be left as an assumption. Knowledge in and of itself is not powerful in any way, shape, or form. For knowledge to translate to something powerful, it has to be applied. In fact, based on your uniqueness, you may learn fifteen or twenty critical nuggets in this book that you find very powerful. Someone else reading this book, because of his or her uniqueness, might find only one or two things worth remembering. Person number one has learned a great deal more than person number two. But if person number one does nothing with all the things she learned and person number two immediately starts to apply the two things she learned, you tell me who got more out of this book. I will say it again: knowledge is not power; knowledge *applied* is power. The reason you have read a form of knowledge applied is power several times already in this book is it is too important, not to reinforce.

The combination of experience and knowledge is skill. For example, when you first get a job, you might have a great deal of experience in that line of work, but you are not necessarily highly skilled in your new company, because every company has its own procedures, its own way of doing things, its own software, its own machinery, its own organizational structures. You also have new supervisors that have their own sets of beliefs and their own ways of doing things. So although you are experienced in the general details of the job, you might have little to no knowledge of the differences in this new company. Once you learn the nuances of the way things work and get to know your supervisor and your peers, your experience plus your gained knowledge equals skill. Again, skill is a critical factor in your uniqueness.

If you're in a supervisory role, if you're a small business owner, or if you're just one of the millions of people out there doing what you need to do, understand that skill in and of itself is a distant second to *talent*, among the most important factors in achieving success in life and maximizing your productivity and happiness and those of your team, your families, and so on.

The most critical factor is talent. Simply stated, talent is the innate abilities within you that allow you to do certain things well the first time you do them. You had zero experience and zero skill, yet you did it well. *That* is caused by talent. Talent can be concrete things like "I could always fix engines" or more subtle, "People always seem comfortable around me." But talent is the secret sauce! Rarely considered and even more rarely utilized, talent is what separates good performance from great performance. People operating in areas of talent have higher levels of initiative and higher levels of engagement than others. They embrace the concept of self-leadership, and they are significantly less frustrated and less drama prone. They almost always are more successful, happier, and more productive than those that aren't working in their areas of talent.

There is no magic formula here for knowing your talent. But think about this: do you like doing things you're good at, or do you like doing things you stink at?

Now I'm going to tackle something that I will write about in much more detail later in the book. But first I have to make one thing clear: the concept of work-life balance is horribly flawed. Now might be a good time for you to skip ahead and read chapter 3, "Traditional Views of Life Balance and Time Management Are WRONG" (unless you like to do things in a linear way, reading page 1 and then page 2 and so on). Here is the simple truth: you don't have two brains; you don't have four lungs; you don't have two hearts; and you don't have two lives. Learn from generation Y that completely separating your work from your personal life is a critical mistake. Life is hard enough and complex enough when you just try to run one. With two, you double the complications—at least. If you get nothing out of this book other than the idea that you have only one life *and* if you begin to function that way and think that way and act that way, your life will be altered for the better.

So as you read the rest of this book, when I skip around from family example to relationship example to work example—please understand that some of you, because of your uniqueness, will see all that skipping around and all that separation as OK. You'll say this is when I'm in work mode; this is when I am at home mode; this is when I am in relationship mode, because many people have more than two lives. They have 345 lives. I am not saying these people are bad or these people are wrong; I am saying with certainty that if you have more than one life in your mind, you are complicating that one life significantly. The chapter called "The Power of Goals That Work" will give you practical tools to prioritize life and work.

I write like I think, a bit all over the place at times. Back to talent. How do we know in what areas we have talent? I provided a simple definition.

I use an exercise we created at the Genesis Group as part of our Talent Maximization System© that can help drill down further. Take a moment to get a piece of paper. Or just write in the margin of this book, or do this in your head. List three or four things you really love to do. Not things you enjoy at work, not things you enjoy when you're not at work—just three or four things you really *love* to do.

I used this simple exercise in 2008 when I was profoundly unhappy in every area of my life, and especially miserable at work. Show me someone who is completely miserable at work that doesn't have a care in the world when he leaves work. There are exceptions: some people have an amazing ability to leave work at work, but they are extraordinarily rare. Typically issues at home manifest themselves at work, and issues at work manifest themselves at home because at the end of the day it's all one life. Here is my list, which I created prior to firing myself from my job in 2008. But these things were on my list before—long before—and they still are on my list today. Why? Because these are things I *love*, and they are ingrained.

- I LOVE being in front of a group speaking.
- I LOVE interacting with people to help them improve.
- I LOVE being active.
- I LOVE doing what others see as impossible.

So I looked at these four things and simply asked myself how these relate to my life. I have to convert everything to practical terms; theoretical stuff doesn't work for me. So when I looked at this list, it occurred to me that throughout my career in the military and after, when I was away from work, I was happiest and most productive when I was doing one or more of these things. I *feel* good when I'm doing anything associated with these four areas, and I feel good in all the different areas of my one life when I'm doing things I love. At home, at work, with friends, with strangers, by myself, it's all good when I'm doing one or more things I love—bet you're the same, one of the few things almost everyone has in common.

Look at the list above again. Now look at your list and ask yourself why you love doing these things. *Why?* is a powerful question, because if you can't immediately come up with a list of reasons why you love each one of these things, you don't actually love them. You might love the items on your list because you've had success; you might love them because they give you a feeling of accomplishment; you might love them because they make you feel good about yourself or feel good about others.

Where there is love, there is passion. If you truly love something, you will not be silent when somebody says, "Tell me why you love it." You immediately know. So the question *Why?* is a very important one to ask. If you find yourself struggling with answering it with one of the items you say you love, replace that item with one for which you can immediately answer that question.

Sometimes we answer the way we think others want us to answer. This not only applies to this little exercise, but also extends to our greater life, as will be discussed in different parts of this book. When we allow other people to dictate how we live and what direction we choose to go in, we are making a fundamental mistake. Absolutely seek the advice of many people you trust and respect, but make your own decisions.

After writing down the many reasons you love these items, build the skills you have accumulated that are related directly to the things you love. Skills include both knowledge and experience. For example, when it comes to interacting with people to help them improve, some of the skills I have come from my time at the US Navy's Senior Enlisted Academy in Newport, Rhode Island. I also have read countless books on self-improvement, communications, career success, and so on. I have more than twenty years of supervisory experience, developing and leading people. I have researched in great detail things such as personality styles, generational differences, and how the conscious and subconscious mind works. And I have applied these things, experimenting with myself and with people in peer groups that I reported to and those that reported to me. So I have an extensive list of skills for helping people develop and improve.

After you build your skills list, build your talent list. If you have done your skills list and made a comprehensive list of the applicable knowledge and experience you have gained, you can go back to this list and find some talents hiding there. In other words, you will have things on your skills list that are neither knowledge based nor experienced based. For example, if I had on my skills list "charisma" or "people trust me," those would be examples of talents, not of skills.

Remember, a talent is inherent to you; it is something you just do, something that causes a certain reaction from people without you doing anything exceptional, or something that allows you to be well above average in an area without having anyskill in it. If one of the things you listed is that you love to cook and you have on your skills list "I know when food is done," you probably also are good at timing meals, and you probably have a good sense for what spices go with what foods. Take those off your skills list. You have lulled yourself into thinking, "I've done it so many times; I've learned these things," so you counted it as experience or you counted it as learning, and you put it on your skills list. Think back to the very first time you cooked, you put together a meal with lots of different dishes and pulled it off pretty darn well. Well, you didn't have any experience in how long things take to cook, did you? You didn't have experience in what spices work well with other spices; you just sort of knew through your taste buds. *That is talent my friend.*

We often bury our talents and write them off as either experience or as knowledge, but remember that talent is something that comes from within. This can be confusing. Say you have experience in public speaking. Your jobs have required you to conduct training so you are an experienced trainer and you are experienced being in the front of a room. Maybe this training has gone fairly well. This is definitely a skill, but could it possibly be a talent? Yes, because those that are truly exceptional at delivering training, at delivering speeches, or at conducting programs have a sense that you can't gain through knowledge or experience. They feel the audience; they anticipate what direction to take the participants.

So you might have a great deal of skill in communicating with others because you have communicated with others your whole life. But you might have true talent for communicating. If you have a *talent* for communicating, you always find a way to adapt your communication so that it is understood by the individual or the group you're talking to. This is a gift; this is a talent. So boil down your huge pot of skills to a few nuggets—a few talents—based on the things you love.

Next look for common themes in your lists. I refer to these as core talents. When I looked for the core commonality among all my talents, here's what I came up with: interpersonal communication, public speaking, insight into people, vision, and an ability to simplify concepts, regardless of how complicated they are. When I did this exercise in 2008, I asked myself a simple question: how can I make my talents the foundation of what I love to do? How can I turn them into something I can make a living at? Well, I combined my list, and what I came up with was talent for communication of all forms and great insight into people.

From here it was easy to ask, "What if I were to create a company that allowed me to observe people, communicated with them, and then help them get the maximum productivity out of the people in their organization?" This is how Genesis Consulting Group, now the Genesis Group LLC, was created. Our tagline is "We Maximize Human Capital." I not only love what I do for a living, but I love the living, as well. Do you know why? If you live one life, everything is easier and everything becomes possible. I often think about an upcoming program while riding my mountain bike and often think of hiking in the woods when waiting for a coaching call to start. One life thinking is beautiful.

The point here is not that you have to create a job or create a company. Rather the point is to be mindful of your talents and seek opportunities in all the areas of your one life to spend as much time in those talents, in those areas you love. If you can't identify your talents, you have little chance of finding a position in a company that you will thrive in. If you rarely spend time doing things you love outside of work, again you have little chance of thriving—one life, one life. We have trouble positioning ourselves so we can get to that magical place called "success" or "achieving our potential in life." My personal definition of success: reaching a place where I am happy and I have peace of mind. But finding out what success is for you—what achieving your potential looks like or feels like—is an individual journey.

Again, the intent of this book is to help you get to your unique potential. It is important for me to throw in a very significant disclaimer here. It is impossible for you to spend 100 percent of your time using your talents doing things you love. The most fortunate among us spend perhaps 65 to 70 percent there, so we all have to do things that we don't like. This is called life, and those of us who live by the concept of one life understand that almost a third of it is going to be doing things that are required and that we don't like. So please do not think this is a guide to Nirvana or a guide to never having a bad day, to never having another war, to never being frustrated or angry. There's no such thing as perfection, but there absolutely is such a thing as peace of mind, satisfaction, success. I know, I am well on my way to being there, and you can be too. So now that you have listed specific talents to go along with the three or four things you love, the logical question is, what can I do to start spending more time in these areas of talent? This is where we have to look back at that word *skill*. Again, skill is the combination of experience and knowledge. You can be the most talented person in the world in a certain area, but if you have no skill to apply that talent, it is not worth much; it is like knowledge that is not being applied. So the key now becomes talent plus skill.

This is a great time for you to do a skills inventory; here is where your uniqueness really comes in. Your experiences and your knowledge are all filtered by your unique personality and the environments and people that have influenced you. So when you consider your skills, you are in fact considering your uniqueness. I encourage you to identify skills in the areas where you have had success. Just because you have a skill does not mean it is in an area you enjoyed or an area where you have been successful. Although many factors can lead to things turning out poorly, in my opinion, it is likely because you were void of talent in that area of skill.

Try to think of skill you have used in a way that has brought you joy or success. I wrote about several of these when I was identifying my areas of talent; they were specific skills that I applied to produce good outcomes. A simple example would be my talent for helping people develop themselves. The skill that maximizes that talent is my study of personality styles, cultures, generational differences, and knowledge areas, and then my application of those when I interact with people. So my natural talent to bond, my talent to communicate, my talent to put people at ease can be fully maximized only if I apply some experience in combination with what I learned about our differences, with the experience I gained applying that knowledge, and with the fact that I have insight into people that many do not have into themselves. So that is how I have taken talent and added skill.

Jack Canfield's *Chicken Soup for the Soul* includes a very powerful formula:

TALENT + SKILL = STRENGTH (expertise over time)

In the business world many of you have likely heard the phrase "maximize people's strengths." The more you can actually apply this, the more you can work, or more precisely live, in a more satisfying and gratifying place. Whether you are a parent, or a supervisor, or just someone people listen to at the neighborhood BBQ, try to get people to live in their strengths. Of course this is only possible if/they actually know what their strengths are, but we have already given insight into how to figure that out. Broken record time here, do not think just work, your talent, your strengths pop everywhere! I like a very neat, proper yard. I'm a "routine" guy. I have my exercise routines. I have restaurants and stores I always go to. But, remember, I love to do the impossible. Talents related to that are persistence and the ability to focus on outcomes first. These form many of my home routines and allow me to make them, well, routine.

All too often when people talk about a strength, they do not understand that a combination of talent and skill produces a strength; that is where strength comes from. When you understand this, you are in a much more powerful position.

A brief note here on the opposite of strengths: weaknesses. We are taught from an early age that we need to focus on our weaknesses. We set aside strengths and we work on weaknesses. At home and at work, it's all about getting better at what we are not very good at. While doing this we let our strengths lie idle and sometimes even atrophy. Bottom line is, if you are to achieve your unique potential life, you get good enough at your weaknesses to be okay or average. Then go back and get *great* at your strengths as soon as possible. Strengths will take you to heights you never thought possible; spending all your time in weaknesses is simply not the best use of your time.

We are led away from our strengths by well-intentioned people that have no clue who we are and what we are capable of. Almost from the day we are born, we start getting categorized; we start getting trained; and we start getting programmed to conform to a specific mold or expectations. Our parents, our relatives, and our friends do this while we are growing up, and later, in and out of the workplace, everyone seems to be hurting us in one way or another because of their desire *not* to hurt us, by molding us to a specific pattern with specific features. We can attribute this to human nature.

Another aspect of human nature is that people like people that are like them. Highly educated people tend to hang out with other highly educated people. Musicians and artists tend to hang around musicians and artists. I was a proud enlisted man in the US Navy, and I spent the majority of my free time around other proud enlisted men and women. There truly is safety and comfort in numbers, but there is a dark side too. At birth, we are a completely unique individual, and almost instantly we start getting pushed to be like others. Maybe our moms read a parenting book, and before we could even speak, we were already being programmed. Some of us went to day-care facilities where we were continuously pressured to be like the other good children. I simply want to stress that *almost every influence in our lives encourages us to be anything but unique.*

Achieving your potential hinges largely on your ability to discover what makes you unique against and amid what almost everyone around you is making you "discover" about yourself. I realized early on in my days in the navy that people looked up to me for direction. In basic training, the recruit chief petty officer that the company commander had put in charge sought me out for advice. I didn't know then why this was so, but he did. I was in the bunk above his, and he would tell me every night after lights out that he did not want to be in charge, but he had never quit on anything in his life, so he wasn't going to quit this job. I coached him as best as I could, but he simply did not want the job. It was evident too that he didn't have the talent for it. I later came to understand that one reason this happened is that people just trust me. I didn't learn this; I didn't get experience in it. People trust me, so they often seek my counsel.

There is only one person in this world that has your combination of talent, skills, and life—you! This young man had lots of skill, a good deal of talent, and plenty of living under his belt, but none applied to the job of running a recruit company in basic navy training. Something else I learned in basic training is that I'm not afraid of failing. (My love for doing the impossible is directly related to this talent.) In fact, I don't even think of failure. When I decide to do something, I just do it. Yes, this has caused me pain and heartache over and over again, and it has led to heartache for those around me, but it has also paved the road to great success.

What follows is a story based on my talent for leadership, which I developed into a talent for fearlessness. As I have told you, my recruit chief petty officer (the navy term for the person in charge of a company in basic training) wanted very much to be fired. He absolutely refused to quit, though he did not want the job, nor was he particularly suited for the job.

We were almost two weeks into basic training, and our company was doing very poorly. He became more and more despondent, and I became more and more convinced that I was the right person for the job.

If you are not familiar with the military, rest assured that what I did next is something you just don't do in the navy. I spoke to our two grizzly, twenty-plus-year company commanders. I told them that the recruit chief petty officer was not the right person to lead the company. When they asked me who I thought the right person was, I quickly responded that it was me. When they asked me why, I told them why. They sent me to what was called MOTU, or motivational training unit.

Keep in mind that this was 1983, and the motivational training unit was run by borderline psychopaths who enjoyed inflicting pain on young men and women for the most marginal of offenses. I was run ragged by increasingly heavy-handed "exercises" for the better part of forty-eight hours with little to no sleep and then returned to my company. Those two grizzly senior chiefs called me into their office and asked me who I thought should be in charge of the company. I told him I was even surer than ever that it should be I. Without hesitation, they sent me back to the MOTU for forty-eight more hours of love and personal care.

When I returned, they once again asked me the same question, and I once again gave them the same answer. Realizing that I was too stupid to understand the lesson trying to be taught, they told me the lesson. The lesson was that you support your leader even if he is marginally competent. I did not bother to tell them that the petty officer in charge had all but made me ask them to fire him; that was not relevant to the lesson. They asked me if I understood the lesson as explained, and I told them I did, and so I was summarily dismissed.

Within twenty-four hours, they gathered the company and relieved the recruit chief petty officer of his duties and made him the master at arms. And they put me in charge of the company. The company went on to enjoy great success; we graduated as the honor company for our basic training unit. And I was selected as the honor recruit from that company.

I share this story not to pat myself on the back but to give an example of the power of taking advantage of your talents. I had a talent in critical areas for the job, period, and so things went well for all of us. I had *no* skill in the areas of running a company of recruits, but with talent, skills grow quickly. Very soon I was pretty darn good at being a recruit chief petty officer.

There's another important point here: if you have talent in an area related to whatever you are doing, you will get very good very fast and will pass those with greater skill but no talent. The combination of skill and talent leads to great personal success. In my case, it also led to the great success of an entire company of young men.

Perhaps an even more powerful example of combining talents with life experience happened after I graduated from basic training. I literally walked across the street to quartermaster A school, where I was going to learn navigation. I had learned navigation much earlier during my not-so-successful run as a cadet at State University of New York, Maritime College. I remember very clearly the first day of what I think was a two- or three-month school. They were going over all the things we were going to learn. I quickly realized that I wasn't going to learn anything I didn't already know. I had learned navigation; I had experience in navigation; and I had talent—a sixth sense for navigation. So navigation was a strength.

I made a request to go see the senior officer in charge of quartermaster training. The request was approved, and when I met with him, I respectfully requested to take the final exam. I asked that, if I passed, could I skip the training and go on to submarine school in Groton, Connecticut. I told the senior officer about my experience and my background, and I told him my request was not coming from arrogance but from my core beliefs that continuing with the training was a waste of the navy's financial assets and, frankly, my time.

The military veterans out there can imagine how well this one went. If you don't have a military background, I assure you it did not go well. Our instructor was a twenty-two-year senior chief coast guardsman, and he was well aware of why I was asking to see the officer in charge and was also well aware of my background and experience. He approached me and offered me the following deal: I would not be required to go to class but only to take the weekly quizzes. Furthermore, if I agreed to run a night study course from four to six each evening for students that were having trouble *and* the class average stayed above 80 percent, I would have no duty and no assignments. Once again, I realized that my talent, combined with experience and the bonus ingredient of risk taking, had led me to a very good place.

A bit more on the military. As much as the military often tried one-size-fits-all policies or rules, I was bound and determined as a junior enlisted man to seek out my unique talents, and as I became a supervisor, I sought out the unique talents of the people around me. What I found out was that this led to extremely high productivity with the minimum amount of stress and frustration. This is not some psychological miracle; it's common sense. People doing things that they are good at produce better results, have higher initiative, and are less likely to be stressed and frustrated. It is in everyone's best interest to spend most of their time in areas of their unique talent.

This simple formula allowed me to move through the ranks, likely as fast as anyone ever had. I have no idea who holds the "record" for the most junior command master chief in navy history. I attained that rank in sixteen years, which I believe at that time was six years faster than average. I had no connections, as I certainly was not and still am not very good at politics, and yet I attained the highest rank for an enlisted person in the navy nearly 33 percent faster than the average. Furthermore, keeping in mind this average, the command master chief represents something like about 1 percent of total navy enlisted personnel. You do not achieve this rank by accident or by sticking around. And you certainly don't achieve it in sixteen years without doing something very differently, and very effectively, this stuff I'm writing about works, please use it to improve your life.

While doing this I was NOT applying any of this to life outside of the navy, and because of that I did *not* excel in life in general. I had not embraced one life, so for every success at work there were failures outside of work, including alcoholism, mental challenges, on and on. In a strange way these issues prove how powerful talent development is. Despite all the baggage, success still came in spades. Once I applied the formula to everything and embraced the one-life rule, success began to come in all directions.

Now, back to your regularly scheduled book.

What I did differently is what I am encouraging you to do: follow your unique talent, recognize it, acknowledge it, claim it, tap it, maximize it, and allow it to lead to your greatest success. I wish I had a dollar for every time I've told individuals and groups that I have only a precious few talents, BUT I worked very hard to become the very best I could be by using those talents as much as possible. Additionally, I tell people that I spend as little time as possible in the areas where I lack talent.

I have tried to live most of my life in the talent zone. And it is natural for me to help others find their talents and turn them into strengths. Do the same in your relationships outside of work. Remember, passion, joy, and life come out of doing things we enjoy and being around people that complement us and our talents.

When I retired from the navy, people thought I was kind of crazy to go into advertising sales for a CBS-affiliate television station, but actually it played perfectly to my unique talents. I was good at communicating. I was good at problem solving and very good at quickly earning people's trust. That pretty much sums up the key characteristics of an outside salesperson. Learning the mechanics of television advertising was relatively easy because I had the talent to sell. I had a very successful career as a salesperson, albeit a short one. However, after about six years of being a sales executive and then a sales manager, and with the twenty years in the navy, I realized I had compiled a great deal of knowledge and experience—that is, skill—in guiding people to achieve their unique potential. In fact, after more than 26 years of working in this area of strength I had become an expert, from this the Genesis Group was born (www.gconsultinggrp.com in case you missed it before).

Here is another way to get to your talents and your passions. Please answer this simple question: if you had all the money you needed to live very comfortably, what would you choose to do? In other words, if money were no object, what kind of work would you do? Also, what are the things you do at work that you never need to be reminded of or that you never have to remind yourself of? We tend to do things that we enjoy first. We procrastinate on the things that we don't enjoy.

This is as good a place as any to let everyone know there is no such thing as the perfect job. Every job has aspects that do not engage our talents. The key is to become competent in our weak areas; we don't have to be great in them. I wrote about this earlier, but it is important enough to repeat. We waste time when we try to be good at something we aren't talented in, and we waste time with others when we try to make them good at something they don't have talent in. If you really want to enjoy living, if you really want to enjoy what you do to make a living, spend most of your time in an area or in areas that you have talent in.

Warning: this can be an uphill battle. So many people still run organizations according to the "experience is key" mind-set. This is fundamentally flawed, and these lost souls unfortunately still make up the majority of hiring personnel. So what choices do you have?

Take your inventory of things you truly love and begin to screen potential occupations based on them. Remember that it isn't just the occupation but also the person you are going to be working for and the people you are going to be working with that have a massive influence on your satisfaction. The more you work and spend time in your areas of talent, the better the chance that you will thrive.

Another option is to create your own job. More and more people are creating jobs; they are becoming entrepreneurs in areas they have a passion for and areas they have expertise in. This is one of the best ways to ensure you are using your talents to their full capacity. I fired my boss and myself in August of 2008, and I set out to create the perfect job for me. It has taken some years, but this job—founder, and initially the chief everything officer of the Genesis Group LLC, helping individuals and organizations reach their professional potential —has become the perfect one for me.

Even more gratifying is creating jobs for people who share our passion and vision.

Now I'd like to provide some thoughts for entrepreneurial thinkers. This type of thinking is part of what makes you unique, and if you do not have the talent for pure entrepreneurial action, then there are other options in which you can still "be your own boss." (That is a joke, by the way, as we all work for someone.)

Do you have the *talent* for being a pure entrepreneur, meaning the thought of starting a company with no money, no prospects, no clients, and no customer's sounds exciting to you? Take this little quiz to see if you might be in this niche.

- Do you constantly think of ways to do something better?
- Are you willing to risk all your assets to turn your thoughts into actions?
- Do you have the will to SELL—knock on doors, live on the phone, network EVERYWHERE, beat the bushes, SELL, SELL, SELL?
- Do you have expertise in an area that you want to turn into your job?
- Do you know why anyone pays for this expertise?
- Do you know exactly WHO would pay for this expertise?
- Do you have the financial resources to survive with ZERO income for twelve to eighteen months?
- Do you understand how brutally difficult it is to keep up the persistent drive needed to have any shot at success?

Well, have I terrified you yet? Starting a business from a clean sheet of paper is extremely difficult. You need

- passion,
- purpose,
- persistence,
- discipline,
- persuasiveness, and
- expertise (in your product or service area, not in starting a business).

Fear not. And stop sobbing if you say, "HECK, NO!" Your unique talents are in other areas. Remember, not just talent in whatever you need to do to make a living, but talent in all aspects of life. Surround yourself and embrace those areas and stop trying to fit that round peg in that square opening called your life. It just never fits and can be rather uncomfortable (slightly off-color sailor humor).

So, what makes you unique? Your talent and experience make the only you there can be. TALENT is your most important asset. You can have all the experience in the world, but without talent, you are never going to be much more than OK at anything. Remember the success formula is:

Talent + Skill (experience + knowledge) = STRENGTH

Stop wasting time in areas that you are OK at and trying hard to become really good at them. This simply does not work. Spend your time in areas you have TALENT in. THIS IS WHERE EXCELLENCE and GREATNESS come from.

Why THEY Don't Get YOU

Make the most of yourself, for that is all there is of you.
—Ralph Waldo Emerson

I make my living as a keynote speaker, author (assuming I actually sell a few of these), and human productivity expert. I assess, interview, and observe individuals, units, and entire organizations. Though I say I make my living as a human productivity expert while referring to my company, the truth is I've been a human productivity expert for my entire adult life. It is one of the prime reasons for writing this book, because I know that anybody who uses a few of the tips and techniques discussed in it will be successful.

Do you want to hazard a guess at the two major issues that adversely affect productivity in nearly every organization I have ever worked in or assessed? They are accountability, which we will talk about more in the chapter 6, and communication. I'm still waiting for the day that I walk in to brief the C-level officers of the company and say the following: "Ladies and gentlemen, after spending four days looking at all levels of your organization; I have to tell you that your communication is amazing.

Your middle managers make sure frontline personnel are aware of what's happening daily, and at the same time your senior-level personnel are continuously interacting with your middle management. The rank-and-file exchange thoughts and ideas openly, not just within their units but throughout the organization. Communication here is completely and totally transparent at all levels and in all areas; it is amazing that everybody understands exactly what needs to be done to achieve the results required of the organization, of the divisions, and of the units." Yeah, right.

And I'd love to hear this in a conversation over a beverage with a friend: "I have the most amazing relationship with my husband. We talk about everything—good conversations, tough conversations. We share our emotions; we share our thoughts; we collaborate and communicate continuously. There's nothing we don't know about each other or our concerns or troubles." Yeah, right again.

It would be irresponsible of me to write a book called *Upside: A Guide to Achieving YOUR Unique Potential in Life* without addressing effective communication—which is in danger of becoming, a lost art. As technology becomes more and more prevalent, our communication skills become worse and worse. Make no mistake: your ability to communicate effectively with others is at the foundation of your happiness, your satisfaction, and your success.

Communication also serves as a superb example of my one-life belief. If you are not communicating effectively with your partner, problems are guaranteed to occur; if you are not effectively communicating with your supervisor, problems are guaranteed to occur; if you are not effectively communicating with your children, problems are guaranteed to occur; if you are not effectively communicating with your peers and with the people that report to you, problems are guaranteed to occur. Effective communication is everything.

The fact is that we are by nature not very good communicators. That's mostly because we incorrectly assume everybody thinks like we do. We assume that the way we communicate will be effective for other people. If you got nothing else out of chapter 1, hopefully you got that every single one of us is a unique individual. Therefore, if you want to be effective in your communications with friends, family, coworkers, and everyone else, you have to change the way you view communication.

Here is a book on achieving your unique potential in life with a chapter that asks why people don't get you. Huh? I'll start with why good communication matters. You have no chance of success, no chance of achieving your unique potential, if you are not effective in your communication. Let's start with those nasty little critters called They or Them. Ever wonder who they are? Things would be so much better if *they* would just listen to me. *They* just don't understand how important this project is to us. We spend a lot of time throwing the *they* word out there, and we are always referring to some people outside ourselves. The fact is that there is one of you and hundreds of millions of *them*. So if you want to have any chance of influencing them, you have to learn how to communicate effectively with them.

The late, great Dr. Stephen Covey, in his book *The Seven Habits of Highly Effective People,* wrote about seeking first to understand and then to be understood. It matters not that his book has been out for twenty plus years and that many look at it as old school. Much of the book is as powerful—if not more powerful—in today's world as it was when Dr. Covey wrote it. Seeking first to understand and then to be understood means this: if we are going to communicate effectively with other people, we must understand their uniqueness first. If we assume they are just like us, we will be wrong, 80-90 percent of the time. Again, one-size-fits-all fits no one, and this is never more critical than when talking about effective communication.

In his groundbreaking audio series on relationship strategies, Dr. Tony Alessandra talks about the Platinum Rule. Most everyone is familiar with the Golden Rule: "Do unto others as you would have them do unto you." This sounds nice; it sounds loving; it sounds caring—but it's just not effective. How can this be? Because when you say, "Do unto others as you would have them do unto you," you are assuming they want to be done unto as you want to be done unto. Nothing could be further from the truth.

So Dr. Alessandra discusses the Platinum Rule, which is, "Do unto others as they want to be done unto." This is powerful. This is where Dr. Alessandra merges with Dr. Covey and his "seek first to understand and then to be understood" habit. For you to communicate effectively with another at home, at work, or anywhere, you have to know that person. I could write an entire book on effective communication and might just do that, but this book is meant to be a quick, handy pocket guide, so we're going to cover three critical areas of effective communication. These are not all the areas, and not everyone will get everything out of these, but they are a solid starting point for you to be more effective in your communication.

The three areas we're going to write about are personality/behavioral styles, generational differences, and effective listening.

Oh my, personality/behavioral styles. This is where I'll potentially lose two-thirds of the readers of this book. I have promised practical advice that you can tailor to your uniqueness, and here I go rolling in personality styles. Notions of D.I.S.C. and Myers-Briggs evaluations and any number of other personality configuration styles, colors, and letters may be dancing through your head. If you have no idea what the heck I'm writing about, you're fine—likely in a better mental state than I am. For the record, I believe D.I.S.C. to be the most effective assessment tool, *especially* with respect to assessing team dynamics.

Regardless of what tool you use, regardless of what Myers-Briggs type you are, and regardless of whether you find the results fascinating or silly, please do not dismiss the origin of the discussion of personality and behavioral styles: Dr. Carl Jung, a psychiatrist in the early twentieth century. Jung studied under the much more famous Dr. Sigmund Freud, but he made a potentially career-ending move by taking exception to Freud's approach to treatment to his patients. Jung believed that in psychology and in the treatment of psychosis, one-size-fits-all fits nobody. (Sound familiar?)

In 1921 Jung published *Psychological Types, Volume 6*, in which he defined four basic personality functions common to all people. These four functions are how people take in information; the other two relate to how people make decisions. He asserted that each one of these functions could either be extroverted or introverted. Key to his study is that all of us have the ability to blend these functions and to move in and out of an extroverted or introverted state. That being said, like a left-handed person, we might be able to throw a ball or scratch our name out with our right hand, but it is not what we are most comfortable with. We are most comfortable with our core functions and our core styles.

According to the Myers-Briggs test, I am an ENFJ. If you have absolutely no idea what those letters mean, read on. The E means I'm an extrovert. Shocker there! The N means I gather my information mainly though intuition, versus pure facts and data. To say it another way, my gut is my main indicator, not just "the facts." I absolutely feel first and think second, so I am an F. And lastly I am a judging (J) person, which means I lead with decision making whereas the other function leads with information gathering. Essentially this is exactly who I am. In the D.I.S.C. world I am an Influencing – Dominant and a very strong one at that. This means that I am a passionate, enthusiastic person that thrives on breaking new ground and getting things done. Again, when you peel the onion on this, which I will not do here, since we do not want any crying (bad onion joke), suffice it to say, it is extremely accurate. I encourage you to take some type of personality test and encourage those close to you in your life (all areas of your life) to do the same. They will provide you great insight into yourself and into others and will make you a more effective communicator. It is a great idea to not just take a test but have the evaluation done by someone who actually understands the meat behind it, well worth the time and any dollar investment that is associated with it. As I wrote earlier, I'm a D.I.S.C. fan, but any legitimate personality profile, and there are many, is better than running around blind.

I wrote earlier about Dr. Stephen Covey's habit "seek first to understand, then to be understood," and this is absolutely applicable to these various personality tests. It is exactly why I encourage you to take one and have those around you take the same one. Although I believe in investing in having a professional help you understand and apply the results, if you cannot afford such help, do not let that be an excuse. There are apps and free online tests for both Myers-Briggs and D.I.S.C. as well as others, so just do it. Type, "free DISC assessment," into Google or your favorite search engine, you'll find several. Understanding others' personalities goes a long way to understanding them, so you'll be on your way. Not only do we have different personality styles, but it is definitely to our advantage to embrace them and to understand them.

Let me restate that almost all legitimate personality tests trace their way back to the Jungian archetypes (personality types). I often refer to personality styles when I'm conducting programs, and when I begin to describe the different styles it always gets an immediate response from the audience. This happens because people begin to hear descriptions of themselves and those they know well. It is almost always a huge "aha" moment.

To have a bit of fun I've created a regular-folks version of the four main personality types. Certainly not thorough and certainly not a replacement for one of the proven, time tested assessments, but I'm going to bet you will read through them and start "seeing" yourself or people you know—almost everyone does. Final word before our first and I think only pop quiz is that most people have a very strong primary trait, a fairly strong secondary trait, and traces of the other two traits. So here we go.

Pop quiz time. First question: Who is Daniel Lawrence Whitney? Second question: Who is Larry the Cable Guy? Third question: What do these two have to do with each other? Final question: Why the heck did I ask the first three questions? Daniel Lawrence Whitney is the man who created and who is Larry the Cable Guy. I start this section with that because my first personality style takes his famous phrase, so I want to make sure I give credit where credit is due. "Git r done" is Larry the Cable Guy's mantra, and it is our first personality style.

Git R Done people are all about being extremely busy and producing results. They are generally considered intense and perhaps a bit cold or distant. Again, since personalities are exposed most under stress, they are typically most easily identified in a work environment. Because of this, I will describe what the different personality styles look like at work. That being said, I do not believe people have completely different personalities outside work. They may consciously force themselves to act in certain ways, either at home or at work, but at their core they do not have separate personalities.

So back to Git R Done personalities. Left to their own devices, their workspace—cubicle or office—will be stark. They are not huge fans of chitchat; they are all about business. If you want to chat with a coworker on Monday morning, this is not a personality style to do it with. They tend to be aggressive in their communication, meaning they are going to speak first and listen almost never. They are interested in hearing a couple of pertinent facts and making a decision. They seem to be happiest when they're stressed out of their mind and borderline completely overwhelmed. Juggling twelve projects is fantasy meets reality for this personality style. Git R Done people don't have a desire to be in charge; they have an absolute need to be in charge. Taking charge and being in charge is something they feel at a cellular level.

The second personality style is referred to as FACTS Please. These people are all about linear thinking. If it's worth researching, it's worth researching for the next hundred years. They love data, numbers, and organization. Their workspace is impeccably organized. They might even have Velcro on their stapler to make sure it stays in place on their desk. Like the first personality style, they are about getting things done, but they are much slower to make decisions. They struggle with decision making because they're always concerned that they may not have all the facts; they wonder if they've spent enough time analyzing the data. People who think that six sigma is better than sex typically fall into this personality style. Yes, I went there.

One of the most significant differences between this personality style and Git R Done is that FACTS Please is a much more passive communicator. So if you come in and ask a Git R Done person how the weekend was, you'll probably get cut off in midsentence. FACTS Please people are much more likely to hear you out, take a long pause—this is their annoyance that you're bothering them—and throw out some type of an answer in the hope of making you move along. Make no mistake; they are as annoyed as Git R Done people, but because they are much more passive in their communication, they handle the interruption differently.

They too will have a fairly stark office but are much more likely to have something cerebral like those teamwork posters that show a bunch of people rowing in unison. FACTS Please people typically are much more introverted than their close relatives, Get R Done folks. They are more likely to want to create the presentation than deliver it.

Next come How Are You people. These are the people with massive empathy. Everybody likes them. They always make time for you; they never have a harsh word for anyone; and they are always willing to help. They are typically quite organized, a characteristic they share with FACTS Please people and to a lesser extent with Get R Done people, but they are much more focused on people than on business. This is an important distinction between this personality and the first two we discussed.

These are the folks that always have two bowls of candy on their desk—one for diabetics. They throw up fake spider webs and have a pumpkin around Halloween and have their workspace decorated to the hilt for the other holidays too. These folks know you're in a bad mood when you open your car door or get off the train in the morning. They are welcoming, caring, and again almost universally liked.

The biggest challenge for How Are You people is that they get taken advantage of because they have an absolute fear of conflict and confrontation. They would rather gnaw their own leg off than be involved in a face-to-face argument. They also typically are not comfortable in doing presentations for strangers. That being said, they usually make very good trainers because of their ability to empathize and to feel the audience.

Remember I talked about how stark the offices or workspaces are for the first two personalities? For How Are You folks, this is very different. Their workspaces are full of pictures of friends and family. And those pictures are there for one reason and one reason only: for you to say something about them. You can see the importance of understanding a little bit about personalities here. When you stop by the offices of the first two people and "bother them" with chitchat, you have made a mistake. But when you don't take a minute for How Are You, you have also made a mistake. He or she loves chitchat.

The last personality style is Let's Talk. These are the folks that absolutely love to chitchat. The difference between these folks and How Are You folks is that they will carry on or start a conversation with complete strangers. They also typically don't really care if the other person is engaged or interested. This is very different from How Are You people, who are completely in tune with who they are speaking with and typically will get involved in deeper conversations only with people they know. Let's Talk people don't care if it's somebody they know or a stranger.

These are the folks that stop by your workspace, and say "Got a minute?" Every inch of your fiber is screaming, telling you to say no, but for some reason you say yes. And thirty minutes later they leave, and you are frustrated and wondering what the heck they just rambled on about.

The reason you have a hard time saying no to these folks, regardless of your personality, is that they are very good at getting people to do what they want them to do. They generally get look details, much preferring the thirty-thousand-foot view. FACTS Please people drive them crazy. They are good at being in charge, but that is not a requirement, as it is for Get R Done people.

These people are natural performers. A very high percentage of successful outside salespeople, trainers, speakers, and entertainers are Let's Talk. Like

How Are You, they have lots of personal things in their workspace. But unlike How Are You, there may be no pictures of friends and family. This personality style loves to have all the awards and recognition that they've received on their walls. When you walk into the office of a Let's Talk person and ask if that is her Brownie sash hanging on the wall, she will reply with something along the lines of "Oh, that old thing," and sort of shrug it off, but the bottom line is it's on the wall for one reason: for you to say something about it.

The better you understand these personality types, the more effective you will be at being understood. When it comes to achieving your unique potential, the better you understand and are open to the differences of those around you, the more effective you will be.

I'm pretty sure I've used this phrase before somewhere in this book, and maybe in the editing process they figured that out and cut it, so I want to say it again here—and this is directly applicable to achieving your unique potential in life: the only expertise you really need to have is knowledge of who the expert is. That means always partnering with people that have talent in areas you don't have. This means they likely won't have your personality type.

When I first got into mountain biking, the friend who introduced me to the sport was a great riding partner for me. He was a lifelong cyclist with massive quads who could churn his mountain bike up the steepest incline, regardless of what the terrain was. I would be gasping for breath, switching back and forth as best as I could, and often stopping and having to walk my bike up the incline, and yet Mike would just churn to the top. Inevitably, though, I would come close to catching him on the downside.

Mike was a cautious, experienced mountain biker who was not afraid of down slopes; he just respected down slopes. I, on the other hand, was always intrigued by how fast I could go on that loose gravel fire trail on a thirty-degree grade. So Mike would dominate on the uphills and I would typically dominate the downhills—on those days that I didn't crash before catching up with him. (By the way, see how nicely my aggressive, little-fear approach to mountain biking fits in my "do the impossible" theme? It's one life, all tied together.) So at the end of the day, when we got back to the trailhead, it worked out just fine.

This has been true for me in business too. The first person I become best friends with, seek out, hire, or influence is someone who is great with details and organization. The operations manager of Genesis is magnificent at scheduling, letter writing, and all other things detail. This is perfect because I'm OK at that, but frankly I don't like it much.

If you are to achieve your unique potential, you must understand you cannot do it in a vacuum. Use this chapter of this book to help you identify your talents and become acutely aware of them and also acutely aware of the areas you have no talent in. Then, rather than trying to get good at something you have no talent for, find someone who has it. In relationships this loosely translates to this: opposites attract. But it's not so much that opposites attract; it's that people with different talents complement each other.

My life partner keeps an impeccable house, is a world-class chef, and sees everything through the eyes of non-emotional thinking. None of those are areas I'm particularly good in. That being said, we also share a great deal, and I think this is a critical point. We both are very mindful of staying fit and of all that comes with wellness. We are both extremely entrepreneurial and find discussions about growing the Genesis Group LLC and the divisions of Genesis fun.

So I would encourage you to look a little past the expression "opposites attract" and see if you can identify complementary talents. A relationship with complete and polar opposites—that is, people who have nothing in common—will very likely not end well. And a relationship in which the couple states, "We are exactly alike; we like all the same things," is likely to hit some BIG bumps as well. After all, a healthy relationship has people in it that have their own identities. OK, once again my rambling mind digresses; now back to the topic at hand.

Another critical difference is that between generations. Never before in our history have we had four generations simultaneously in the workplace. Before you read another word, please understand that, though we are grounded in one personality style, we tend to move a bit among styles when we go through life changes, career changes, or personal experiences.

Before I discuss the generational differences, again know that I'm using generalities. My son acts nothing like others in the generation he is part of, but my daughter is almost a prototype for her generation; they are two years apart and were raised in the same environment. Do not think of the exception to these general guidelines and throw out the guidelines. Remember, our goal here is to be more effective in our communication, and a key to effective communication is to better understand the people we are engaging with. When you know nothing else about the person, you have never heard him speak, and you have never been around him, all you really have is a first impression. If you have a general idea of that person's age, there are great benefits to understanding generational differences.

A superb book on this topic is *When Generations Collide*. If you are fascinated by what you are about to read, I encourage you to get that book. Because we are all different, you might dissect every person you know and try to fit everyone into a personality style and a generational style. Or you might almost pooh-pooh that as unimportant. To each his or her own, but I will tell you this: my experience both personally and in the observation of countless highly successful, happy, fulfilled people tells me that learning more about personality styles and understanding the generalities associated with generational differences can be a key to your success. What follows is a very broad overview of generational differences. Again I recommend the book for those of you interested in a much more detailed view.

Traditionalists were born between 1925 and 1945. Not many traditionalists are active, or at least not visibly active, in the workplace today, but they still have a massive influence on the organizations and companies you work for. They were raised to work hard, to appreciate everything they have, and to be extremely loyal to the employer that was kind enough to provide them with a job. The traditionalists are the parents of the early baby boomers.

Baby boomers were born between about 1946 and 1965. It would be almost unfathomable for you not to have heard the term "baby boomers." They are the largest generation ever born—about eighty-one million strong—and if you look at the events that have occurred during their life, you see that they have been on the front of the wave of social change, technology advancements, and many, many other changes. For the most part, they were raised in a traditional household: Dad worked, Mom was at home, the boomers went to school, they came home, they sat at the breakfast table, they had a cookie and a glass of milk, and then they were supervised as they immediately did their homework. If you are old enough to remember this word, most baby boomers had chores—specific activities that they were required to do to "earn their keep."

Boomers were bombarded with the importance of education, hard work, and loyalty. They were raised in an activity-based world, were told what to do, and responded without question. In fact, many boomers can probably remember the advice they got when they went for their first job interview: say "yes, sir," and "no, sir," and when they ask you if you have any questions, the answer is no, because only troublemakers ask questions. Since boomers were raised by traditionalists, there was no generational issue in the workplace for years and years and years, because both the traditionalists and the boomers had the same view of work: work hard, be loyal, and keep your mouth shut.

Along the way something interesting happened: baby boomers decided if one income was good, two would be better. For the first time since the necessity during World War II, women in massive numbers joined the workplace. Dual-income households became the norm rather than the exception. Along with this came the inevitable stress of two people working different shifts, spending less time together, and seeing each other less. Divorce rates skyrocketed, and single-parent homes became almost typical. Children were being born and raised in a very different world than that of their baby boomer parents.

Generation Xers were born between 1965 and 1982—a tiny generation of approximately forty-six million. This generation is significant for several reasons we will talk about shortly. Unlike their baby boomer parents, who were raised with strict supervision and oversight in an activity-based world, a great number of these children were latchkey; they were coming home not to Mom but to an empty house. What they learned at a very early age was that as long as they kept their grades up, as long as they didn't bother the neighbors, and as long as the dog got fed, they could do whatever they wanted to do.

This generation created results-based thinking. These were the first outcome-focused people. The baggage that came along with this was a chip on the shoulder about nobody ever being available to go to school event, to watch the play, to go to the baseball game, to cheer them on in gymnastics, to see them in choir. So they grew up largely alone and focused on results.

If you look at the large difference in ages in the workplace that have been present for more than one hundred years, isn't it interesting that it was not until the mid 1980s that generations started to get mentioned?—about the time generation Xers joined the workplace. Before this, there were no generational issues, because the generations in the workplace thought and approached work identically. This ended when gen Xers were told that they had the job and they needed to be there at 7:30 on Monday morning. They asked, "Why?" Both Generation X and Generation Y, after them, have been asking why ever since, often to the great frustration of their Baby Boomer bosses.

Of course, this was heresy to a baby boomer or a traditionalist, but it was a logical question for an independent, results-focused gen Xers. They reasoned that if their job was data entry and they had a clear understanding of what they were responsible for producing in a given week, what did it matter when they came in and when they left? This is a brilliant question, and one that baby boomers and traditionalists really do not have an answer to. The reason they do not have an answer is because for thirty or forty years they never questioned what time work started, what time they went to lunch, what time they had to be back from lunch, and what time the day ended. Generation Xers have been making decisions for themselves since they were twelve or thirteen years old. Now they're twenty-two, and a baby boomer is telling them what time to go to bed. This does not sit well with them.

A gen Xer is also much more likely to ask questions such as, "I understand what your expectations of me are, but I would like to know what this company offers me. What's in it for me?" Many baby boomers and traditionalists see this as selfish when in fact it is simply payback time for gen Xers who have never had the spotlight on them. Their most prized possession is control of their time. They are not necessarily interested in the organization or in their co-workers, but they are extremely interested in control of their time, because they have had it since a very early age.

If you are working with or around gen Xers or have friends or neighbors in this generation, you will be well served by figuring out how to help them gain more control of their time. At work, this is the key to higher productivity in a gen Xer; in other areas they will thank you for your brilliance in helping them control their time—their life. If you are a classic gen Xer, use this knowledge to work better and understand your frustration.

Also know that this is your time; every day more gen Xers are running the show and fewer baby boomers are around. You are replacing a generation nearly twice your size, and you ARE in the driver's seat. Flex hours at work, day care, and home shoring (working from home) are ALL products of gen X. Congratulations! It will only grow as you gain more authority.

As generation X grows up and as the baby boomers get around to having their second round of children, you have two generations contributing to this next generation. What we call tail end baby boomers were feeling guilty about not spending enough time with their older children because they were working all the time. And generation Xers are classic hover parents who never had any attention paid to them, so they're going to make sure they pay all their attention to their children.

So the generation being born from the tail and baby boomers and the generation Xers is generation Y, or the millennials. Born between 1983 and 1999, they are seventy-seven million strong, only slightly smaller than the largest generation ever—the baby boomers. Unlike the generations before them, they grew up with an iPhone as a baby rattle. Baby boomers were blown away by the advent of color television. And generation Xers experienced the World Wide Web for the first time, albeit through something called dialup. A gen Xer was excited when a picture could be downloaded while he or she slept overnight. That's not the case with gen Y, with its instant gratification and knowledge of the world literally at its fingertips.

Because of the guilty baby boomers or gen Xers with their stolen youth, gen Yers have a unique trait: they are going to have *everything*. It's all about social; it's all about fun; it's baseball games where there are no winners and losers; everyone gets a trophy. This was the huge social experiment of generation Y, almost a utopian generation in their early years. They have the results focus of gen X, but they see no separation between work and play; they see everything as life. Of course I subscribe to this, but only after learning it from gen Y later in life.

Listen closely to the millennial generation. There is more bad information out there on them than all other generations combined. With respect to work they are not lazy, they are not undisciplined, mostly they are 20 something and so much of their behavior is age related. They value leadership and they value clear direction as to what needs to be done, the result. What they want is the freedom to get there how they chose to get there. The most tech savvy generation they make up 30% of the workforce. In 10 years it will be 75% of the workforce.

Gen Y believe work should be enjoyable and it should be meaningful. They are also the most socially aware generation and want to make a difference in the world. None of this precludes generation

Y or generation X from being highly effective employees, but they are not going to get things done the way baby boomers did it. Baby boomers would be well served to work with gen X's and gen Y's natural tendencies in addition to their work ethic. A blended approach would be much better.

My one-life philosophy comes from gen Y. My results focus was ingrained in me but is very gen X. And I have the work ethic of a baby boomer. Hybrid characteristics! If you are a baby boomer, you will be more effective in your communication if you understand these generational differences.

Do not underestimate the power of generation X and the power of generation Y. These generations have two significant factors: one, they are younger than baby boomers; and two, baby boomers are exiting the workforce. Each day gen X is becoming more and more controlling of the workforce, and gen Y is becoming a critical component of the workforce. If you are looking to maximize and achieve your unique potential, you must be aware of these critical generational differences within your family, your workplace, and your community.

This is worth writing again here: if you are a baby boomer and still doubt the power of generational differences, ask yourself how much day care there was at the first facility you worked in. In 1980 how many people worked virtually, and how many companies allowed employees to engage in volunteerism on company time? All of these are products of gen X and gen Y.

Make no mistake; good economy or bad economy, the future is gen X and gen. Y. They have significant differences, but they share one common focus: producing results. Baby boomers were raised to focus on activities. If you are a gen Yer or a gen Xer who is supervising baby boomers, do not try to force them out of their routine. The structure and the discipline of going to lunch at noon is core to a lot of baby boomers. Again, do unto others as they want to be done unto.

Gen X prizes control of their time, flex hours, flex travel. They have no issue producing great work, but they want to do it on their schedule. Gen Y loves coaching, personal attention, interaction, and social environments. Understanding and using these critical differences will help you communicate more effectively with everyone in your life. The benefit to you is more effective communication, more effective results, and less frustration.

The last area of the big three of effective communications that we'll cover here is listening. Do you learn when you talk, or do you learn when you listen? I think you would agree that you learn when you listen. So if you want to be an effective communicator, you must be a good listener. One of the most common factors in relationship issues is one or both partners complaining they are not listened to. If you want to be more productive, more satisfied, and less frustrated, you need to be a good listener. Early in my navy career I heard an expression: a complaining sailor is a happy sailor. But the word is not really *complaining;* it's actually "a bitching sailor is a happy sailor." Venting (complaining) is a way to relieve tension. In the incredibly high-stress environment of submarines, there was lots of venting.

When we vent, someone is listening—or at least there's the impression someone is. When people feel that someone is really listening, it calms them; it makes them feel better, even if the listener does nothing more than listen. This is a universal truth, since listening works everywhere—it's not unique to sailors. As long as people feel they are being listened to, actually having attention paid to them, they are almost always going to be more agreeable and more likely to be open to your thoughts, ideas, and recommendations. Listening does not come naturally to me; talking does. I have worked very hard to become a good listener—very hard—and "good" will be where I stay. Being a *great* listener involves talent (specifically patience, something I do not have much of). So I'll just accept that.

Notice I often use the word *accepting;* this is very different from *agreeing.* If you are familiar with the Serenity Prayer, you understand the difference between agreement and acceptance. When you understand someone, you accept what they are saying; you don't necessarily agree with it. The Serenity Prayer is a cornerstone of the Alcoholics Anonymous twelve-step program and helped transform my life. Here it is:

God, grant me the serenity to accept the things I cannot change, the courage to change the things I can, and the wisdom to know the difference.

The most powerful word in that very powerful prayer is *accept*. When you can demonstrate the ability to listen fully to another person and to accept what she says, you have gone a long way in making her feel better, in making her feel less agitated, in making her feel as if she is not alone—even if you do not agree with a word she said. You can have a massive positive impact on another human being by not saying a word. In fact, unless you have some very specific talent combined with some skill in the areas of counseling and coaching, you are best off keeping your mouth shut.

So, listening, as a part of effective communication, is a critical piece of living a fulfilling, enriching, and happy life. Let's dig a bit deeper to give you a better understanding of this crucial topic. There are actually four different types or stages of listening:

Nonlisteners. This is exactly what it says it is. You are not interested in anyone else's opinion: "If I want your opinion, I'll tell you what it is." Nonlisteners always have the answer, are never interested in input, and don't need other people's ideas. If you are honest with yourself, you know you have been a nonlistener in the past or are currently a nonlistener. I assure you, it is impossible for you to reach and realize your unique potential as a nonlistener. This is absolutely, universally true for one simple reason: nonlisteners have no allies. Going through life without allies and thinking you're going to reach a happy, peaceful, fulfilling place is insanity.

Selective listeners. Selective listeners are in every aspect of our lives, hearing what is to their benefit and missing what they are either not interested in or do not see as beneficial. You know a nonlistener, and the emotions you feel when you think of that nonlistener are not positive. Feel free to e-mail me and correct me if I'm wrong. I would suspect you also know selective listeners. Although teenagers have a PhD in this, it is not just teenagers who practice selective listening. In fact, we are *all* selective listeners from time to time. We are best served if we spend as little time as possible in this mode. At the end of this section, I will give you some very specific advice on how to ensure the communication you have with another individual is effective—meaning both of you leave with the same meaning. This will force nonlisteners into a listening mode and will force selective listeners into a more effective listening mode.

Evaluative listeners. Evaluative listeners think they are good listeners. They start to really listen to the person who is talking to them, but at some point their mind starts to formulate a response, a defense, or a reaction. If you are an evaluative listener, you might not interrupt the person, but you mentally stop listening to her. We do not have dual core processors that allow us to listen completely to a person and at the same time process a response or formulate a reply. So evaluative listeners might start off effectively listening, but at some point the switch flips and they stop listening and start thinking of how they're going to respond. Sometimes they do this because they feel defensive or they feel attacked. Sometimes it's because they're caught off guard by a question or they are trying to think ahead about how to reply. In the end, they stop effectively listening. Evaluative listeners have the right spirit of listening, but they cannot stay tuned long enough to listen effectively.

Before I write specifically about the powerful listening mode, effective listening, I want to share the things that make it impossible to listen at all. The only way to effectively listen to another person is to eliminate all distractions. You cannot be typing and listening; you cannot be texting and listening; you cannot be watching television and listening. You cannot be talking to one person and listening to another. You cannot be on the phone with one person and listening to another. I feel like I am reciting *Green Eggs and Ham.* "I do not like green eggs and ham, I do not like them, Sam I am; I do not like them in a box, I do not like them with…"

Effective listeners. So those are things that effective listeners do not do, but what are some things that effective listeners do? First, effective listeners maintain eye contact, but they do not stare. Eye contact proves that you are paying attention. Eye contact without a break is staring, and staring to most people is uncomfortable and creepy. So maintain eye contact but avoid staring. I'll share a bit more on how to do this effectively in a bit.

Second, an effective listener asks open-ended questions when needed. An open-ended question is one that cannot be answered with a yes or a no. Open-ended questions stimulate the other person to begin to speak.

Third, once the person begins to speak, you intervene in one of two circumstances: to bring the person back to the topic or to sum up key points or action items that the other person has mentioned, so you capture and clarify them in the moment. There is no need to interrupt the person to do either one of these. We can talk for only about sixty to ninety seconds without having to at least take a breath; when a person pauses—however slightly—to take that breath, this is when you either interject and bring them back on point or sum up key points.

I'm fairly certain you can identify with this. I can identify with it because I'm usually the person wandering off. When someone wanders off and takes that inevitable break to breathe, so that he can continue to ramble on, say something like this: "I'm hearing what you're saying, John, but I'm not sure what its relevance is in our conversation about what we're going to do about our neighbor's dog pooping in our yard." That was a fairly formal reply to what is more than likely a conversation between partners, but it serves the purpose. The point is not to be demeaning or derogatory, but to bring the person back to the topic being discussed.

Now, here is how to clarify a point when a person takes that inevitable pause to breathe: "So, if I understand you correctly, Susan, we can't proceed until we have approval from engineering that the blueprints meet code."

Susan has been talking for sixty seconds and has said a whole bunch of other things, but you believe that was the key point. After you make your statement, wait to see in the first case if Susan agrees that that was her key point.

Fourth, an effective listener takes notes. I use an iPad; others use a notepad; others use yellow sticky notes; others don't use anything at all. I would say only the last group is in trouble. It is very difficult to remember key points if you do not take notes. Please do not mistake note taking with transcription. If we are trying to capture every word coming out of the other person's mouth, we are not effectively listening. As effective listeners, we listen intently for those sixty or ninety seconds, and when the speaker breathes, we sum up the key points. If the person acknowledges those are the key points, that we understood them correctly, write those points down in the form of a brief note.

Now, some people are taken aback when you take notes, as they think they are being recorded; they think it is going to be used against them. So it is a good idea to let them know right off the bat why you will be taking notes. Here is a superb point that I recommend everyone make a mental or physical note of and apply immediately: *when you explain why you're doing something in terms of its benefit to the other person*, it will be accepted and embraced by the other person. Here's an example: "Susan, I just want to let you know that I use my iPad to take notes when I'm having a discussion with someone. I do this because I don't want to waste your time by missing a critical point that you make. That way I don't have to come back and ask again. Does that make sense?" This is a great way to put people at ease, letting them know that the only reason you're taking notes is to make sure you get it right. This is also the answer to what to do with your eyes so that you aren't staring. Make eye contact for a bit, and then take a note or review your notes. Bam! Issue of potentially creepy staring gone, key tip, take a note here.

The last thing that effective listeners do is ensure when they have a conversation with a child, with a peer, with their mate, with their boss, or with anyone else that at the end of the conversation, somebody sums up the key action items. When talking to a teenager, say, "So, what did you get out of this conversation?" When talking to a peer, typically whoever is in charge of the project and whoever requested the conversation should sum up the conversation at the end. When talking to a subordinate in a work environment, ask for the key takeaways. When talking to a boss, somebody you report to, sum up the key points whether she asks for it or not.

Think of what happens when you finish a conversation with another person. It often ends with something like, do you understand? Or, are there any questions? If you think about it, neither one of those ensures that the person understood a thing you said. This is a massive source of frustration, a massive source of conflict, a massive source of misunderstanding—and completely avoidable. Once again, if I get the sense that I am dealing with a particularly temperamental person, I do not want him to feel that I'm being derogatory or that I don't trust him. I tell him I don't want to waste his time with incorrect information or with having to come back and ask for a summary. Either I give a summary or I ask him for a summary for the same reason. I want to make sure we leave completely understanding each other.

How many times have you been in a situation where a ten-minute conversation turns into a week and a half of useless work? All this could've been avoided by a simple thirty-second summary at the end of the conversation. If we apply this to the one-life concept, these are the same conversations you have with your spouse or partner, the same techniques you use with your children, and the same techniques you use with friends and neighbors. Everything in this book is not just for work, not just for social settings, not just for home, but for all of life. The same techniques, the same advice, the same methodology is applicable to everything because you have one life.

Why Traditional Views of Life Balance and Time Management Are WRONG

My son, Perry, had been playing soccer for years, but I almost never saw him play in a match because I was almost always gone at sea. He was getting ready to play in a select tournament somewhere, and my submarine was in port. Perry was very excited that I was finally going to be able to go to a match. Perry is not an excitable young man and he was not an excitable kid, but he was excited that I was going to be able to see him play in that tournament, and it felt good to see that excitement.

Saturday morning came, and I got an early call from the boat (submarine sailor language for a submarine). Something was a mess—I can't remember what it was—but I had my priorities all screwed up as usual. I told Perry I had to go to work. To this day, and this happened many years ago, I remember the look on his face. I likely always will remember it. Within a few weeks I had completely forgotten what was so important at work. That tells you that I clearly made a bad choice. And this is, unfortunately, one of a thousand times I made the wrong choice. Someone else could have cleared that mess up—or not—but no one could have been a father for my son that time but me.

Screw "balance"! Get your priorities straight, John!

I've always been better at business planning than planning personal things. I spent most of my adult life working too much and playing too little. One day I heard about a life-balance seminar. I remember it catching my attention; the very idea of having better balance in my life was intriguing to me. So I ponied up whatever the cost was and went to this all-day workshop. I probably should have picked up on the fact that the very haggard, somewhat disheveled-looking man sucking mightily on a cigarette outside the hotel where the workshop was might be the facilitator. The gentleman looked stressed, sick, tired, and, frankly, like he was living on borrowed time. Yet he was the facilitator for this life-balance workshop. Beautiful.

As most people do at seminars, I flipped through the pages of the workbook and looked at some of the tips and pointers. The workshop began as most workshops do with a brief introduction of the credentials of the facilitator, and then the smothering onslaught that I call Death by PowerPoint began. The best thing about the workshop was that it took less than fifteen minutes to understand how fundamentally wrong the entire premise of life balance and its next-door neighbor, time management, are. The workshop was worth EVERY PENNY, since it quickly allowed me to see that our approach to "balancing" life is all wrong.

As I wrote in the introduction, do not read stories or lessons learned in a business environment as career lessons, just as you should not read a personal story and apply it just to home life. You see, *that* is the fundamental problem. Trying to balance life by treating work and life as two separate things will never work. It's not work-life balance, my friend; it is prioritizing your life.

What is written on the pages of this book applies everywhere for the simple reason that you only have *one life*. If you are reading this because you have two separate brains and two separate hearts in your body, you are excused. If you have only one of each, not just understanding this but living it, is one of the most important points of this book. I know I've already written this, but I am writing it again. I was into my forties before I had even sniffed the idea of paying attention to my life outside work with the same passion, intensity, and interest as my work life. I read amazing books like *The Last Lecture*, *The Four Agreements*, *The AA Big Book*, *When God Winks at You*, *A Chosen Faith*, and others. The more I read, the more I learned I already had many of these beliefs and understandings inside me. Of course I did, I had just stuck them in the "spiritual" pigeonhole or the "wisdom" box, or the "self-improvement" pile.

The truth is *all* of these and so many other books are about living—period. All of the wonderful things I took away from those books were absolutely applicable to ALL aspects of my life, yet none would ever be on the shelves in the business or career section of a bookstore. In fact, if I had to pick my top five "business" books of all time, only two would be business books: Covey's *Seven Habits of Highly Effective People* and Max Dupree's *Leadership Is an Art*. The other three "business" books would be *The Four Agreements*, by Don Miguel Ruiz, *The Last Lecture*, by Randy Pausch, *and A New Guide to Rational Living*, by Dr. Albert Ellis. I also find that some of my favorite "business" books have great advice for my personal life. Why? You know why: there is only one life. So when you learn something that you use and it helps you at work, do it at home and vice versa. In summary, there is no life to balance, because you have only one life.

Now back to the previously started story about the life-balance seminar. This guy was GREAT! He awakened me to ALL of this in fifteen minutes of painfully boring PowerPoint slides combined with a fifteen-year-old workbook. Wow! I disappeared on the very first break and felt without question that was an exceptional time-management move on my part.

When you think of life balance, what comes to mind? Your professional life on one side of the scale and your personal life on the other, correct? The issue that I have with "life balance" is that it misleads you into thinking that you have these two lives to balance. This is simply not true. The reality is that you have one life; we all just have one life. Getting up, going to work, coming home, doing whatever, going to bed, getting up again—these are all one-life events. Living is actually being in control of your life. Living is when you realize you have only one life and you need to act accordingly. So don't balance; prioritize.

I got my butt kicked for years for not understanding living. My priorities were all screwed up because I was always trying to "balance" work and personal stuff. Guess what? Work always filled the top eight or nine slots of my top-ten list of things that I needed to do. I was not living. I was just plodding through life. Isn't life hard enough? Why complicate it further with two calendars, two sets of books" You will likely never be able to balance life until you forget about balancing and just start prioritizing.

Get rid of the two-calendar system, the two-notebook system. Merge everything. You have one life and only one life. What are your *most importants* for next week? Not what are the important things you have to do professionally and what are the important things you need to do personally. Instead, what are the most important things? Some weeks might be heavy on work, others on personal, but there is only one list. Build it and live by it.

You just read two words: *most importants*. In *The Seven Habits of Highly Effective People,* Dr. Covey wrote about a habit called "Do first things first." This was and is all about doing what's important. When I first saw his simple four-quadrant grid, I was blown away. Instantly I could see where everyone wastes time:

> Quadrant 1—Important and Urgent
> Quadrant 2—Important but not Urgent
> Quadrant 3—Urgent but not Important
> Quadrant 4—Neither Urgent nor Important

URGENT! Hair on fire! Got to get done NOW! We almost always hop to urgent things, but are they important? When you read chapter 4, "The Power of Goals That Work," you will better understand that many activities are just that—activities. They do nothing to contribute to the necessary outcome. How can this be? Pretty simple, really: we do not look at the outcomes. Another habit from Covey's book is to start with the end in mind. Wow on that one, but hold that thought.

So, this book is a practical guide to achieving your unique potential in life. And control of your time is key. But most of us simply do not have a clue as to what needs to be done and what doesn't. So where do you start? Well, chapter 4 talks about goals, which are very important. So stop reading this mess and go read that chapter now.

Go ahead I'll wait.

If you have not noticed, I'm referring to the number-one best-selling business book of all time, *Seven Habits,* but I'm not talking about how to use it in business. I am talking about how to use it in *living* and in setting priorities, not just for being more productive at work. Yes, some of these can be related directly to work and others will be you or family related, but they are all about living one life. Do so and be well on your way to achieving your unique potential in life.

Please remember that goals are your roadmap to ensuring you don't lose focus on the most importants. But as with everything else, if you don't know what the most importants are, that's probably because you don't know what the endgame is. If you start anywhere but with the end in mind, you are guessing as to direction, needed actions, and relevant decisions. Everything comes into question. It will be pure coincidence if you wind up anywhere near where you wanted to be.

By the way, when you get "there" without knowing ahead of time where "there" is, have you arrived or are you lost? Hmm. Once you get the concept that you have but one life and you have but one list of priorities, you may realize that there will be periods of your life when most of those priorities will be either career oriented or personal enrichment oriented. And there's nothing wrong with that.

If, however, you are always trying to find five career things and five personal enrichment things to make your priorities, you are not working off the master list. The questions you must ask are, what's the outcome? And, where do I want to be? Then you can pinpoint the most importants to get there and use goals to make sure that you stay on track.

I don't believe you can have a discussion of life balance silliness without also talking about a very closely related topic: time management. I have no idea how many books have been written on time management. I don't know how many time-management systems are out there. But there are multitudes. Some people love them. Some people find the yellow sticky/blue card method fabulous and wonderful for them. But the entire concept of time management is completely flawed.

I know, stop taking everything and turning it upside down, John. I wish I could leave it alone, but I can't. Many people never achieve their unique potential in life because of these incorrect, bad advice "systems" that fail at their inception. Time management is flawed because it starts in the wrong place. The majority of time-management techniques and systems are all about becoming more efficient with the use of time by organizing better, by prioritizing better, and so on. They're all about getting more done in the same amount of time or in less time.

Now, this feels good, but there are some fundamental issues with it. In addition to time-management systems starting in the wrong place—efficiency—they have a one-size-fits-all approach. The reason some people find certain time-management systems wonderful and other don't is because we are all different. So rather than endorsing a particular system for achieving your potential, I encourage you to throw it all away and come up with your own system based on your talents and skills—that is, your strengths (expertise over time).

The first thing you do is related to what we just talked about: prioritizing based on the one-life concept. Do not start with the thought of being efficient; start with the thought of being effective. Only those who start with effectiveness have any chance of owning their time. So, what's the difference between starting with effectiveness rather than with efficiency? It's simple, and it goes back to the one-life concept and to what you want to be doing a year from now.

Now, when you read about goals in chapter 4—or reread it, for those that skipped to it already (I would have)—you'll see that we will go further than one year out, but for this exercise, one year works fine. Consider where you want to be a year from now: what does is it look like, feel like, taste like, smell like?

Come up with very specific numbers or other clear measurements as to where you're going to be twelve months from now. Some of these might pertain to your career; some might be personal; some might be a blend of the two. It does not matter. Remember, we have one life.

We start there, and from there we examine our present list of activities and ask ourselves a simple question: of the activities I am routinely performing now at home and at work, which directly move me closer to where I want to be? If you are like most people, what you're going to find is that somewhere between 30 and 50 percent of what you do daily at work and at home has nothing to do with where you want to get to. So guess what? People who want to own their time throw these things away.

You might be thinking, "It's all well and good, John, but I don't get to pick what I focus on at work; my boss does. My boss tells me what to do, and I do it. At home my kids, my spouse, my pastor, Ronald McDonald, whomever, or whatever controls my time, not me." Yup, some things that draw on our time are beyond our control, but there are massive amounts of time you could control if you chose to. People that are successful at achieving their unique potential don't stay in victim mode. Instead they are proactive. If you summon up your leadership mind-set, which I believe we all have, you can lead your boss in many instances. I have a life-experience PhD in leading people senior to me; I have never been the senior person, but I almost always "get my way."

You can do this by making the most powerful of all appeals. It starts with "I need your help." It is followed by a call to action to your boss to identify the two or three most important things you need to stay focused on, so that you can best serve the company and her. Talk in terms of the benefit to *them*. All too often we talk about how things are going to benefit us. Appealing to someone in terms of how something would benefit you is never as powerful as appealing in terms of benefits to them. Yes, this powerful strategy works with family, works with friends, even works with those darn little people we call our children.

If you can get the top two or three most importants from your boss and the inevitable "crisis" occurs, you simply say, "I was working on the Bennett project [one of the most importants identified your boss identifies earlier], but I will set that aside and work on this. I won't be able to get back to Bennett until tomorrow." Sometimes your boss will say, "Drop Bennett for now and get on the new project!" But often you will get, "No, that Bennett project has to be done tomorrow afternoon." So will this work 100 percent of the time? No, but it will work so much more than just "eating it" or trying to bull your way through it, which guarantees more interruptions and more urgent projects that are not at all important.

Even if it works three out of ten times (with practice your success rate can get to about six out of ten), that is three times you don't waste your time, and you actually lead your boss. Again, this will not work outside the workplace all the time—and, frankly, if your most importants never align with your family's, you have relationship issues. But enough, I'm no Dr. Phil. Just sayin'.

By the way, if you are in a management position or in charge at home, what I like to call a household manager, I suggest you use the exact same tactics when speaking with children, neighbors, anyone—absolutely anyone. The best way to engage anyone, regardless of where they are in the food chain or who they are, is to engage them by mentioning the benefit to them. A critical part of this is using the three most powerful letters in the world. No, not S-E-X, but Y-O-U. When you talk not about how nice a dress looks, but say, "YOU look so nice in that dress," you are speaking a powerful, benefit-to-them language. "I've heard Marvin's is a very good restaurant; we should check it out" is nowhere near as powerful as "I think you would love this place called Marvin's; they have fresh seafood. Do you want to check it out?"

Let's move on to another major issue with time: interruptions and, much more importantly, what you can do about them. The three major sources of interruptions are people, the phone, and e-mail. In an office environment, we get interrupted every seven minutes on average. The interruption lasts about two minutes and it takes our brains about two minutes to refocus on what we were doing before the interruption. Guess what? You are three minutes away from your next interruption. This is why we get more done an hour before everyone else comes to work than we do the rest of the day. When you come in early, you can focus on a specific result and you have no interruptions.

Let's do something about interruptions. Often we get interrupted by people we report to; they have us stop what we're doing and do whatever—immediately. We like our jobs, so we stop what we're doing and we do whatever immediately. The majority of these interruptions are urgent, but they are not important. We do them anyway because our boss said so. It is neither effective nor career enhancing to fight back or to get mouthy with your boss. However, if you have had effective communication about the three or four most important results you want to achieve and you're working on one of those results, you can say something that sounds like this: "I understand you want this done immediately. I'll stop working on the briefing for the CEO for tomorrow morning, which is what I'm working on now, and I'll get right on this. I just want to make sure that you understand I may or may not get to that briefing draft now." That's it. You're not complaining, you're not whining, you're not rolling your eyes. You're making a statement of fact. It is called assertive communication and it is a game changer.

All too often though we say nothing at all, and this is a fundamental mistake. We know we are being asked to do more than we can ever achieve, yet we do nothing to prevent it, and then we complain. This does not work all of the time, by any means; in fact, depending on who your bosses are, who your coworkers are, or who your spouse is, and most importantly, how effectively you deliver this using assertive communication. I guarantee you, the simple method I suggest above will work more than never, which is exactly what you know happens when you do not try this approach. If you want to see change in others, you need to change first. Let me write that again; it feels so good and is so important that you do not want to miss it: *if you want to see change in others, you need to change first.*

Here are some more tips to control interruptions and be more effective in living your one life. If it is your job to answer the phone, by all means do so. If you are in charge of others and have an arbitrary rule that no matter what is going on all phones will be answered by the third or fourth ring, you are making a mistake. Again, I am not talking about external or internal customer service if you are dedicated to that as your main activity. I am talking about the majority of us, who are conditioned to answer everything. When you do this you immediately become less productive, both in what you were doing before you answered the phone and in being completely focused on who is on the other end, So instead of getting two things done, you will actually get neither done, or at best get two things done half baked, not so good. There is a breakthrough in technology called voice mail. Crazy system, but boy does it allow you to be more effective. It reduces interruptions AND allows you to return calls all at once. Things do not get slowed down when you utilize voice mail properly; they speed up. We trick ourselves into believing that when we immediately answer the phone, we immediately address whatever the issue, question, or whatever is; thus we believe we are being attentive. We believe we are being...wait for it...efficient. We might be attentive, but we are anything but efficient.

The majority of calls do not result in a "closed case." We have to research, to get answers to one or more of the questions—and on and on it goes. Often phone tag ensues; we exchange two or more attempts to contact, leaving powerful voice mails like, "Bob when you have a moment, give me a ring." If you listen to voice mails in scheduled blocks and prioritize them using the Four D method I am going to share with you very soon, you will significantly reduce interruptions, improving your productivity immensely while reducing the frustration that comes from interruptions.

Now, what about e-mail? Again, we have somehow trained our brains that famine, plague, locust, and who knows what else will occur if we take more than five minutes to respond to e-mails. Just as with the phone, when we stop what we are doing to reply to an e-mail, we by definition become both ineffective and inefficient in what we were doing and in the e-mail, because we are distracted. As you do with voice mail, check your e-mail in batches. You may be thinking, "Tell my boss that." Buy him this book and highlight this section, and I *will* be telling him.

Exchanging numerous e-mails over several days, each providing an additional piece or a new request, is neither effective nor efficient. When you sort and prioritize your e-mails in batches, you are more focused, more effective, and, yes, more efficient. I check mine three times a day. I receive about one hundred e-mails on business days, every day. When I started getting e-mails many years ago, I checked them every thirty minutes and panicked between checks. So, yes, I know this takes getting used to. Now I check e-mails just three times a day, and many of those days I'm in an organization conducting interviews, making talent assessments, giving a speech, coaching a small group, or facilitating a four-hour program. Although I typically get between 100 and 120 e-mails *a day* that matter, in some form, my inbox never has more than fifty e-mails in it at the end of the day—and typically more like twenty. Try it, it *really* works.

How? The Four Ds. They are *delete* it, *delegate* it, *delay* it, or *do* it. Again, one-size-fits-all fits nobody, so you may check more frequently or less frequently, so you want three Ds or six Ds. All good. As long as you do something other than instantly answer the phone (again, unless you are the person to answer incoming calls) or instantly reply to e-mails, you are on the right track.

Oh, by the way, I have combined my voice mail checking and e-mail checking recently, and so far so good. I dedicate a thirty-minute block in the morning, at midday, and late in the day to check voice mail and e-mail, to make quick callbacks to set appointments, and to send replies to e-mails. It has been very effective because I have time to think about the important and urgent e-mails and voice mails, typically responding in my next "block" while at the same time quickly doing something with those that are not. When you come across me at a book signing or at a program I'm conducting, ask me to show you my iPhone calendar; these are on there. Again, nothing theoretical here. These are practical tools that can and will change your life if you actually modify them to fit you and then use them. So here we go, the Four Ds.

DELETE IT. If the voice mail or e-mail is neither important nor urgent, delete it. If you are not sure, delete it; if you guessed wrong, the person will call or e-mail again.

DELEGATE IT. If someone else is working on the project or is the expert and if you have built proper relationships, pass along the information to her for action. Now, if you're thinking, "Good luck getting my coworkers to go along with that," look in the mirror. I have rarely come across anyone not willing to help me as long as I have always made myself available to help him.

DELAY IT. If it is important but not urgent, immediately put it on your calendar with a specific note on what exactly needs to be done, why, and by when.

DO IT. If it is no more than a one-minute phone call or thirty-second e-mail, and I will be able to completely address the question or concern, I do it immediately. Leave a detailed answer on the voice mail, not "Sue, give me a call when you have a minute." Those messages are annoying to most and useless to all.

There you have them: the Four Ds. Modify them if you feel they are not right for you, but keep the spirit: blocks of time and a specific system so that you are handling almost all e-mails, personal interruptions, and phone calls just once. That gives you ownership of your time.

Allow me to sum it up very clearly: life balance is one life, one calendar, one list of priorities, one set of goals. Your friend in achieving your unique potential is time ownership. Why? Because, like life balance, time management is also gaga. Remember, if you really want to own your time, do not start with being efficient; start with being effective. Once you have mastered being effective, use the tools we have talked about in this chapter however you see fit.

Yes, I'm beating a dead horse and I will continue to beat a dead horse. You create a system that works for you. My techniques are not your techniques. My methodology may or may not work for you, so I share specific examples. But everything here must be tailored to work with your unique talents, your unique skills, your unique strengths. If you truly start living one life, clearly define your most importants, and learn how to control interruptions, you'll have a very good chance of living a happier, healthier life.

The Power of Goals That Work

So much has been written about goals—so many methods, so many reasons. We think about goals. We talk about goals. We write them down. We carry them around. We do all kinds of stuff with goals, except one pretty important thing: we do not actually get around to following them.

Staying focused is a challenge for me—and not only because of chemical issues in my brain. Without goals, I would never—and I do mean never—get much of anything done. Again, consider Covey's habit number two: "Start with the end in mind." Where do you want to be in five years? To get there, where do you need to be in three years? And to get there, where do you need to be in twelve months? This is where you start. And don't forget one-life living; there is no such thing as a personal goal or a professional goal list. Create only one list that includes your long-term, mid-term, and short-term goals—not others' goal for you.

Do these change? You bet they do. We constantly face things beyond our control. So these are not written in stone, but they are your guide to staying on point to get done what you need to get done. Here are some examples of goals that most anyone would have said I could not accomplish, but I did:

As mentioned earlier, when I was an E-3 in the navy in 1983, I set a goal to be an E-6 within five years of service. It was mathematically possible, but most told me that I could not do it and it would never happen. But I came up with goals to reach at five years, three years, and twelve months. Then I started working on the qualifications and all the other pieces to get to that twelve-month goal, to set me up for that three-year goal, and so on. I made E-6, "first class petty officer" in navy lingo, four years later—a year ahead of my goal.

When I divorced, I took 100 percent of our unsecured debt. Although my company, the Genesis Group LLC (www.gconsultinggrp.com—yup another shameless plug, but what the heck, I'm writing this thing, aren't I?), was still in year four of that critical five-year "80 percent don't make it" range, I vowed to have ALL the debt paid off in three years. So even without any guaranteed income outside of my massive military pension, I made this my goal and then worked back twelve months, and then I figured out what I needed to do monthly to get there. Well, I have revamped that goal, several times, and now can tell you it was all paid off in less than two years. Well over $100,000 of unsecured debt gone in about two years. All of this done by just taking dead aim on one piece and hitting it until it is gone and then moving on to the next. Thank you Dave Ramsey, "Total Money Makeover", rocks. Goals work if you work them!

Another powerful part of goals is that every one of them starts with an overall outcome that speaks directly to what the benefit is to achieving that goal. The outcome that drove my first goal was simple. I noticed that if you were a sharp E-6 in the submarine force, people left you alone; you had a good deal of freedom and control but not too much visibility—a pretty good place to be.

After my divorce, I wanted to get that debt weight off my back; it was crushing me. I'm not a quitter, so although bankruptcy certainly was in play, I wanted to look back and say, "I did it!" No, I don't think people that declare bankruptcy are bad or lazy or quitters. Remember we are all unique and for me, paying all the debt off, was the necessary and right thing.

Oh, and here is a really good tip for those looking to get out of debt: I mentioned one of these books above but here it is again, along with another outstanding one; buy and read Dave Ramsey's *Total Money Makeover*, as well as Thomas Stanley and William Danko's *The Millionaire Next Door*, a book by a couple of really bright guys that look at the spending and lifestyles of high-net-worth people. Ramsey's book is geared more toward people with debt issues, but certainly everyone can benefit from it. *The Millionaire Next Door* brilliantly debunks many incorrect assumptions about how people develop significant wealth. So, until you buy those two books (cash, check, or debit card only, please), here are some really good tips:

- Stop getting further into debt by not spending money you don't have. Do not take the example of the federal government; it will end badly for you. Keep one credit card, and get rid of the rest. If you don't have cash, you go without. Need a new couch? Save for it; when you have the cash, buy it. The same goes for clothes, shoes, and even cars. Stop spending what you do not have.
- Do not pay yourself first; pay your savings account first. Pay the minimum on everything until you have at least three months of net living expenses (including your debt), then move on to the next step.
- Forget paying the highest-interest-rate stuff first. You need cash, so look for the biggest bang for the buck. Let's say you pay $150 per month for car insurance for you and your son. It's a six-month policy, and you have three months left. If you have the money, pay the last three months off. This frees up $150 a month now for the next two months. Dump that extra $150 on your credit card bill. Pay the smallest to largest off, not the highest to lowest interest off. You need some wins, and when things show a zero balance, you are winning.

OK, I digressed. But I'm back with another one of my goals: getting my MBA. I do not like school. I have never liked school. And I never will like school. I just do not like it. As the Genesis Group grew, I needed a higher credential than a bachelor's to be seen as an expert in my area. I was working eighty hours a week trying to get this startup going, combined with big changes going on in my life. But I needed to get it done. So I put a plan together with very specific goals to get my MBA by the fall of 2012. This was a three-year plan that included research, tests, applications, blah blah blah. Well, guess what. I finished my MBA in July of 2012, three months early.

Goals work if you work them. They do not work if you hope they work. They do not work if you are not focused, disciplined, and persistent. But if you are and you have clear goals, they do work.

There are countless ways to write goals. Following are mine. I have no idea who created SMART goals but they have been around forever for a reason: they work. Again, they work if you work them.

First, write the outcome: Why you want this and what it looks like. When writing your outcome statement, think about the benefits to whoever will be affected by the outcome and be involved in the goals. Here is the template I have used for more than twenty years.

S pecific
M easurable
A ccepted/A ccountable
R easonable
T imeline

Example of a poor goal: I am going to start my MBA this year.

Example of a SMART goal: I am going to have my MBA completed by September 2012.

See how that second goal was specific and measurable? Further, I had accepted it and I was accountable for getting it done. I found it reasonable, and it had a time limit on it. Now, in order to get this done, I needed to figure out where I needed to be in 2011 and in 2010.

Do you notice anything else about these two different ways of writing a goal? The first one was about starting; the second was about finishing. Starting something is an activity; finishing something is producing a specific outcome. People that achieve their unique potential focus first on the outcome, not on the activities.

Take a few minutes to write down the three or four results (outcomes) you want to have twelve months from now. Remember why you want to achieve them and, most importantly, the benefits of producing each result. Then write SMART goals. They need to be very specific, using the format above, but it matters not how many of them are career oriented and how many of them are personally oriented, because you have one life. Some people find it helpful to look at each part of a SMART goal as a question and write down the answer to each. In other words:

First, "Specifically what action steps will produce this outcome?"

Second, "How am I going to measure both along the way and at the end to see if I got there?"

Third, "Have I gotten the commitment/input from those responsible for making this happen, and is someone specifically accountable?" This is so critical. Do you, or do the people who have to actually do the work, "own" the goal, or was it just shoved down your throat or their throats?

Fourth, "Is this specific goal reasonable; is it going to be tough but possible to achieve?"

Fifth, "What are the timelines or dates this goal needs to be completed by?"

Note: The last two are connected, so they need to be answered and written in conjunction with each other.

Again, have a single set of goals, not one list for personal and one list for career. But if they are all career oriented or all personally oriented, you may need to examine your priorities. Limit the number of *big* goals to no more than three or four. Now I will tell you what I do with these three or four things, but they may not be what you do. Outside of limiting the number to no more than four, modify my technique to suite you, and how this best works for you. Goals that are not used are useless, just like any knowledge that is not applied. I ask, "If this is exactly where I'm committed to be in twelve months, where do I need to be in three months to be positioned to get these things done in twelve?" I write those down using the same format as SMART goals, and then I simply say, "If this is where I need to be in three months, what do I need to do next week?" At this point, I'm not looking at my five-year goal. In actuality I have five-year, three-year, and one-year goal results I want to see five years from now, three years from now, and twelve months from now.

Some people find that five-year or even three-year goals are too far out; other people I know have ten-year goals. Each one of us is different, but if you have one goal to get through today and that's it, you probably need to push the envelope a little bit and look further ahead. So once I have my four-month goal—or I should say my three-month goal—I just look at my three-month goal, and that is what I use to schedule my most importants for the following week. The most importants are about six items that I have to get done the following week in order to stay on track to reaching my three-month goals.

What I've done here is take perhaps a very aggressive twelve-month vision and turn it into bite-size pieces. What stops so many of us from achieving our unique potential is seeing the result as too daunting. We say, I would like to have thirty thousand dollars saved in the next two years. And we are overwhelmed because we make only forty thousand a year and we have bills and we have commitments and on and on and on. We look at it closely and know we technically could save that much money, but it just seems so hard.

But take that two-year goal. If you need that much money saved in twenty-four months, what is your goal for twelve months? Take that goal and divide it into what you would need to save in three months. If that's all you have to save in three months, what would you have to do next week? This is when you realize that if you make lunch instead of eat out three days a week, you can bank the savings. And if you do your clothes shopping at those large discount stores with the same labels as the much more expensive stores and you only buy what you need, you can save.

You would never look at the long-term goal and say, "I'll start making my lunch." You have to start at the outcome and work back; that's when small, simple things that add up to huge change will reveal themselves to you. So, instead of saying, "My goodness, where on earth am I going to get thirty thousand dollars?" you're now saying, "Next week I'm going to make my lunch instead of buying my lunch out." Anybody can do that, and believe it or not, little things like that add up to big things, like saving thirty thousand.

Feeling overwhelmed prevents us from meeting big goals. For some people, it might be writing a book. Consider how I wrote this book. Initially I didn't follow my own advice; I said, "I'm going to have a book written in two years" and I started writing. It was daunting to me as I wrote and I wrote and I wrote and I wrote.

Then I remembered my own advice, and this is what I put on my calendar: Monday write ten pages in the book. Tuesday write ten pages of your book. Wednesday write ten pages of your book. Do I meet every deadline? No; in fact, this section of this book is being written on a Thursday.

When you schedule your most importants in the first part of the week, it does two things for you. First, you get the unpleasant things done first. Some things are no fun; that's why you haven't gotten them done already. When you postpone them, you dread them all week. So just get them done first thing.

Second, things come up that are beyond our control; they're called life. When you schedule your most importants for Monday and Tuesday, you have the rest of the week to make them up. You don't have to come in early; you don't have to stay late; and you don't have to work weekends to get your most importance done. Yes, broken record time: do the same thing with home projects, shopping, and so on.

When I did this, I wrote the entire draft of the book in a few months. I realized that the voice recognition software did not exactly hit a home run, and my editor really could not edit much of it. I thought I was done, but I actually needed to go back and rewrite the book. Again I did a bit here and a bit there. And soon it was January 1, 2013, and I had rewritten or rough edited only forty-five pages. Back to SMART goals, John. I wrote outcome statements and SMART goals on January 5.

Outcome statement: To help others achieve their unique potential and the happiness and peace that comes with it, you need to have this book done and published. stop being selfish Vincent. (Yes, I'm a bit altruistic, but an effective outcome statement needs to speak directly to your core.)

From that came a SMART goal:

Book will be completed, rough edited, and/or rewritten and delivered to Kathy by me so that it can be easily read, understood, and properly edited by Kathy no later than February 15.

From there I sat down with my Outlook calendar and input blocks of time every week to do nothing but edit.

Editing was done, and the complete book was delivered to Kathy in four weeks.

Before I created that specific outcome statement and then SMART goals to drive the outcome, months passed by with only forty-five pages done. With a proper outcome statement and SMART goals, 150 pages got done in four weeks. And, oh, by the way, everything else that needed to get done still got done as well. Last comment on Outcome statement to goals to next week's most importants. Never have more than 6-9, most importants, in a week. If you have more than 9 go back and review your priorities. It will be nearly impossible for anyone to complete more than 9 most importants, effectively, in any given week, do not try to be the exception.

Take Three *P*s and Call Me in the Morning

Do not go where the path may lead; go instead where there is no path and leave a trail.
—Ralph Waldo Emerson

Nothing great was ever achieved without enthusiasm.
—Ralph Waldo Emerson

No, not those kind of *P*s. These are the kind of *P*s that seems to be present in all people who have found, or are on the road to achieving their unique potential in life.

First some background on where the three *P*s came from. One of the most amazing petri dishes for studying people is the world of submarines. In my nearly fifteen years on operational submarines, I had countless hours to observe all the different personalities and all the different styles of leadership, management, and communication. I got to see people with wildly different talents and wildly different skills, and therefore wildly different strengths (expertise with time).

Remember the powerful formula: Talent + Skill (the combination of knowledge and experience) = Strength. Spend at least ten thousand hours in an area of strength, and you have found true expertise. OK, the ten thousand hour number is a guideline. If you think of a ten hour day that is one thousand days operating in your area of strength to become and expert so roughly 3 years. Not exact but a good rule of thumb. Conversely if you remove talent from the formula, one hundred thousand hours spent in an area will still not result in expertise. Talent is the single most significant factor in developing strengths and eventually expertise.

Long before I started to research this, I began cataloging all these variables. I then tried to identify what separated people just getting by from those people that achieved exceptional results for themselves and for others, in all areas of life. I took copious notes; I made numerous observations; and almost nobody on any of those submarines had any idea that they were part of my little science experiment. Everyone was included in my observations.

I had the privilege of serving with exceptional commanding officers, such as Capt. Brad McDonald, who taught me as much about leadership, in the 18 months we served together, as everyone else and every book I've ever read in my life combined. But in a completely different way I learned nearly as much from a young seaman. A seaman is a very junior enlisted person in the navy. I was a chief petty officer (think middle manager) when I first met this seaman, who changed the direction of my life. This seaman was not very well thought of, not very well liked, and very close to having his time in the navy come to an abrupt end. But he had many of the same traits as Capt. Brad McDonald and many of the same characteristics and talents as I had. But I was a rising star in the submarine world. Two men literally at complete opposite ends of the seniority scale, the responsibility scope, and the experience meter, yet he and I shared very similar qualities—especially talents.

I went out on a bit of a limb and challenged this young man. My approach was based on my observations of him. He was a very prideful person who had learned that aggression, both verbal and physical, was the best way to protect his pride. I never would have had this conversation with most people, but when you can speak to a person as a unique individual, you are speaking to him in a way he understands—and powerful things can result. What follows is our conversation as near as I can remember, word for word. Clouded by nearly twenty years of life between then and now, it is as close as it can be to how this critical verbal exchange happened.

It is not easy to find privacy on a submarine, but we did in a place called the sonar equipment space (SES). I told this young man that he and I had many similar characteristics that were not welcome in the military: independent, resistant to authority, outspoken, unafraid of discipline. These were obvious in both of us. Yet I was one of the fastest-rising men in the entire submarine service and he was a few months away from a general or less-than-honorable discharge.

I asked if he knew why, and he said no. I told him, "The difference is I am the best at my job. Nobody will ever study harder or learn more; nobody could ever practice and research more; and nobody will ever out produce or outperform me—nobody. I am the best at something. You, on the other hand [here is where I tapped into his pride], do none of that. So at the end of the day, I'm a high-potential—though eccentric—sailor, and you're a punk with a big mouth."

He verbally pushed back hard; that *punk* word angered him. I stood firm. "The difference between you and me is nothing more than I'm great at something, and other than being a pain in the ass, you're great at nothing. So, yes, you are a punk."

I then asked a simple question: "Do you want to be a punk?"

He lowered his head and softly said, "No, I want to be great at something."

"At what?" I asked.

"Navigation, I want to be great at navigation."

"What does *great* mean?" I quipped back. And I very clearly saw that pride gene take over. He stood up straight, looked me dead in the eye, and with teary eyes and a bit of a shaky voice said, "As good as you."

To break the tension of the moment, I broke the ice with, "Be better than me, Cory."

That young man went to work that minute, became one of the finest sailors on that submarine, and went on to receive a commission (he became an officer). He has taught navigation at the Naval Academy and continues to climb the ranks. He is achieving his unique potential and he has done every bit of it. All I did was ignite a spark, a spark I saw and felt in him but was not sure he knew he had. You can do the same in your life and you can do the same to inspire other should you so choose.

I was asked by a small-business owner at a workshop I was doing once, "How do you make people care?" My response sums up the exchange with Cory I just shared. "You can't make people care; you can only make them aware of the benefit to them of changing their behavior. The rest is on them."

I learned from many others in the navy—wise men and wise women that were extremely successful with respect to achieving their unique potential. And, even more importantly, they had an exceptional ability to help and develop those around them.

My study of people has never been limited to those around me professionally; I study everyone. There are thousands of people at hundreds of cocktail parties, bars, social gatherings, and block parties, walking down city streets or strolling in a park, that had no idea they were in my petri dish. Some people fascinated me; many others did not. I was all about looking for common threads in people who seemed to have found happiness, success, and a peace of mind and who really seemed to be getting where they wanted to go, not where others wanted them to go.

Yes, you can "see" peace of mind and you can feel happiness, so you do not need to talk to or interview people; you just need to be in tune with our instinctive ability to feel others' energy. You have it; we all have it. But most do not tap into it—instead; they ignore it, never taking time to develop it. Since we are unique tapping into this ability is easier for some than others but all of us can do better than we presently do. It may never become strength but just being OK in this area can be a game changer in achieving your unique potential in life.

I'm going to take a brief stop here to tell you my definition of *success again*. Success is happiness and peace of mind. Of course, that is my definition, and if I asked the thousands of people reading this book what their definition of success is, I would get thousands of different answers. Therein lies my point: do not let any anyone else define what your success is. You define your success. It matters not how you define it, but I do think having a clear definition is critical to achieving your unique potential.

Now, I could write much more about the components of happiness for me and the things that have to be aligned for me to have peace of mind. Obviously my definition of success—to be happy and to have peace of mind—sounds vague to anyone reading those words. That's OK; the last thing you want to happen and the guaranteed way for you to never achieve your unique potential in life, is to allow someone else to define your success.

So, I observed successful small- and large-business owners and midlevel and senior executives that seemed to be happy and grounded. I looked at other salespeople that were professionally successful and at the same time enjoying what they were doing and enjoying their life. I observed couples together for forty-plus years that seemed to love each other, often referring to the other as their closest and best friend. I've spoken with hundreds of people that just "feel" calm; they look and act vibrant and excited about life. These are people that have achieved or are achieving their unique potential. They are first and foremost their own person, following their own path. Yes, many have people in their lives—partners, spouses, friends, children—that enhance them, but at the core of each of these people is a love and respect for themselves, and a satisfaction with themselves. They are truly happy in their own skin.

Was this an objective and quantitative assessment? Absolutely not. Life is neither objective nor quantitative. One of my talents is the ability to read people and almost to feel as they feel. Interestingly this talent diminishes as I get to know somebody better. I am most effective at evaluating people I have just met or simply do not know, sometimes understanding them and what makes them tick at an almost cellular level, even when they are complete strangers. The closer people get, the less accurate my reflections and observations are.

When working with clients I often refer back to my initial notes, thoughts, and observations to bring me back to center. With the fact that I feel first and think second in mind, this actually makes quite a bit of sense. We all feel first, but I really feel (emotional response) and spend more time there than most people. Through years of practice, I believe I have developed a strong link to that part of my brain. As I get to know people, I more quickly push through the feelings and spend more time thinking and analyzing. So I often trick myself into rewriting first impressions. I encourage you not to do this. That does not mean your first impressions are always correct and that you should not be open to people changing or that you simply were wrong, but challenge yourself to hold on to first impressions, yet be open to the possibility that people change as well as that you might have misjudged.

Finally we are getting to the subject of this chapter. (Darn, John, I thought that ADHD had eaten you up.) Let's explore the three *P*s: purpose, passion, and persistence. Truth be told we have been talking about the root of this chapter all along, just using different words.

People who are on a clearly defined path that seems to be fulfilling to them or who have arrived at whatever goals they set for themselves seem to have *purpose, passion, and persistence*. They may have reached their destination; they may be at a stopping point before heading out for their next destination. To me, these people seem to be at peace with themselves and with where they are going. I looked at this as objectively as I could, and then I considered other people that, for whatever reason, were frustrated, upset, or felt unfulfilled. They did not meet my definition of success, which may not have been their definition of success, and they certainly did not have peace of mind; they did not seem happy. They were all missing at least one of the three *P*s, if not more. So it occurred to me that for people to achieve their unique potential, they need all three.

Here are descriptions of the three Ps, listed in order of importance:

Purpose. Some people call this an agenda, the endgame, the ultimate goal, or results, but I call it purpose. If I get in my car and want to get "there," what's the first question that comes to your mind? Where is there? Before you start going someplace, don't you want to know where you're going? If you are to achieve your unique potential, you have to know where you're going. You need to lead a life and live a life of purpose.

In Rick Warren's book *The Purpose Driven Life*, "purpose" is a Christian-based, God-focused purpose. The book has sold over thirty million copies, so I'm guessing that *purpose* is pretty powerful to many people. In fact, God is an important part of my purpose, but I am advocating no such specific focus here. Your purpose is unique to you, but searching your heart, your spirit, and your mind for your purpose is a journey well worth pursuing. My purpose has changed and morphed over the years; I think yours has as well, or it will. With most of us, maturity, life events, and "stuff" (what I called living scars) tend to cause us to have shifting purposes. Here is what I believe is my purpose at this point:

To use my talents for communicating and connecting with people to fulfill what I believe is God's will for me, to help others help themselves.

This latest life purpose came out of my continuing journey of sobriety and broader mental health. It has been more than ten years since my last drink. As I worked through the twelve steps of Alcoholics Anonymous, the eleventh step kept kicking me in the back of my head. It reads: "Sought through prayer and meditation to improve our conscious contact with God, *as we understood Him,* praying only for knowledge of His will for us and the power to carry it out."

About eleven years after first reading the eleventh step, it has become the basis of my purpose. Wow, when you have purpose, you really do have a reason to get up and get going every day—and that feels great.

People that achieve their unique potential live with a clear purpose. Sometimes your purpose is a stop along the way that spawns a new purpose. Other purposes, like mine, are never really achieved; you just want to get close enough to almost touch it.

Passion. You can have a great sense of purpose, but if you are lacking passion, one of two things will happen: 1) You will give up because you never really "arrive" at your purpose—but without passion, what is going to fuel you?—or 2) you will fool yourself that you have achieved your purpose, that you have arrived and no more work is needed.

Passion is the fire that fuels the mind, body, and spirit. To achieve your unique potential in life, you must be driven by passion. I talked earlier about three or four things you love to do; there is passion associated with things you love to do. That's why I emphasize the word *love*. That's why I did not say to list three or four things you don't mind doing. Or list three or four things you like to do. Things you love to do have passion attached to them.

There is a misconception out there that passion is always found surrounded by talent. This is not necessarily the case. One of the things I love to do is gardening & landscaping. I have a true passion for gardening, and I hope I always will. I love to create something where there was nothing. I love to create a little habitat for bugs, birds, and squirrels, whatever. I love to help things grow and develop, both people and plants. So I have a passion for gardening.

Unfortunately I kill almost as much as I help grow; I do not have a green thumb. So passion does not always have talent as a friend. Conversely you might have a great deal of talent for something but not be particularly passionate about it. Because of my insight into people, I have been able to help and advise people on personal decisions. When I have advised on decisions and people have chosen to follow that advice, those decisions have turned out to be very good for them. So I believe I have a talent not just to have insight into people but to offer them advice.

This makes sense, and it follows my one-life concept. It would make no sense for me to have a great sense for people when it comes to their careers but no sense when it comes to their personal life. That being said, I have great passion for helping people develop professionally and I have great passion for providing the tools to help them to develop personally, but I do not have the passion to be a marriage counselor or to be involved in spiritual coaching and things along those lines. I am envious of those that have both the talent and the passion in those areas, but I do not.

Remember, passion is the fuel that will keep you driving. It will fuel your pursuit of your purpose. And passion does one last critical thing for you. Without passion, you are going to have no help along the way, no real fans. Passion fires up not just you, but also others. You get support; you get buy-in; you get true teamwork—all fueled by passion. It will also fuel the final *P*, persistence, and help create a fire for persistence in others as well.

Persistence. Purpose is your reason to get up every day and get going, and passion gives you the fuel to make things happen. But without persistence, you will likely fall short. Why? Well, mostly because purpose and passion in and of themselves do not produce results. You need an action component to go with them, and that action component is persistence. Purpose gives you the focus to work toward something that matters, and passion keeps the fire burning. But persistence gets you through life's roadblocks.

When I was in broadcast television sales, I told my sales teams to get a yes or get a no, but never settle for a maybe. If you get a yes, good for you; if you get a no, that was a no for today for that particular product or opportunity. Give it a month and go back after it again. Purpose and passion are simply not enough; you need to grind and grind and grind. That is persistence. Persistence has many things associated with it. This is where goals come into play, because they will help you stay on track and remain committed. Focus (purpose) is critically important here. You can be extremely persistent, but you can be persistent in doing things that have nothing to do with your purpose. You can waste passion (fuel) being so very persistent on the wrong things.

I see this professionally all the time when I go into organizations and observe extremely busy people working fifty, fifty-five, sixty hours a week. Their coworkers and their bosses refer to them as the hardest-working people they have and are often crushed when I say, "Yes, but they don't get anything done." So persistence without purpose can be a waste of time.

Persistence means a day never goes by when you are not working toward your purpose. This is in no way saying we do only things related to our purpose, but if you have alignment with the three *P*s and combine them with some of the other tips and thoughts in this book, watch out, world! Here you come! If you really want to explode (in a no messy, good way), there is one other factor that is a massive multiplier in truly moving toward *your* unique potential in life.

Expertise. We are a society that has come to love experts—and for good reason. When you have true expertise, your decisions are better, faster, and produce better results. Expertise in highly specific areas has replaced "jack of all trades," and jack is not coming back. The three *P*s are life guides. You have but one life, and if you live it with purpose, passion, and persistence, you will be on your way to achieving your unique potential in life—and developing your expertise.

When I talk about expertise, I am talking specifically about career expertise. Management has been flawed forever by this idea: let's figure out what people are good at and let's figure out what people are bad at. After we do this, we invest time and money and energy and everything else to help each employee get better at what she's bad at, and we abandon the further development of what she's good at. If you want to develop expertise in yourself or expertise in others, you must focus almost exclusively on what you and they are already good at.

Expertise comes out of prolonged work in an area of strength. That's why you have seen this formula throughout this book: Talent + Skill =

Strength (expertise in time). Without talent, there can be no strength. Without skill, the combination of knowledge and experience, there can be no strength. So once you have strength in something, and you continue to grow and develop, you gain expertise. (By the way, true expertise, like true potential, is actually never reached; it is a lifelong journey.)

For the years Tiger Woods dominated golf as it has never been dominated before, and in my opinion will never be dominated again, (I know about Byron Nelson's run of 11 straight wins in 1945 but keep in mind many talented golfers were off fighting the war) he was the poster child for the three *P*s combined with expertise. He was the true expert in his niche. Arguably, he was one of—if not *the*—most talented golfers of all time. What most people either do not know or have forgotten is that he was also a student of the game. He inspired every professional golfer to pay attention to their physical conditioning and strength as critical success factors to the game. He studied, he learned, he applied. Remember, knowledge is not power, but knowledge applied is. Nobody practiced harder, nobody knew the game better, nobody studied better, and nobody researched better than Tiger.

Here's what almost everyone saw in Tiger Woods:

- Tiger's purpose—to win more majors than any golfer in history.
- Tiger's passion—destroying the competition, not just winning but also dominating.
- Tiger's persistence—practice, refine the swing, hit the gym, get back to the range, work more with the golf psychologist, and live, eat, and breathe everything needed to achieve that purpose.
- Tiger's expertise.

Unparalleled talent combined with his unparalleled skill gave him strength. Persistence took him to expertise.

So if this is the winning formula, what happened to Tiger? Many now wonder if he will ever break the all-time majors win mark that few doubted he would in the fall of 2009. In fact, most thought it was going to be easy for him, given what he had accomplished to that point: fourteen major championship wins in just eleven years.

Then his very public, very ugly extramarital affairs came to light, along with the very public breakup and divorce. We very quickly learned that apparently Tiger was not focused on a single goal with purpose, passion, and persistence. We found out he was an actual flawed human being, just like you and me. Tiger Woods has not won a major since 2008 (as of March 2013). Yes, he is still one of the best golfers in the world, but he is not "Tiger" anymore.

This is the other side of expertise and the three Ps. I love Tiger Woods, and I continue to hope he can regain the focus he once had and win more majors than anyone in history. Why? Not because I dislike the golfer who owns the record, Jack Nicklaus. I love him too. Not because I want Tiger's detractors to have to eat crow; I have no interest in that. No, I want him to get there because I need to believe that when life gets in the way of our purpose—and life always gets in the way of our purpose—we can regain form and get back on the trail to our purpose and beyond. Another wonderful outcome of what happened to Tiger would be if he finds a new purpose, whether he shares it or not, and takes that passion, persistence, and expertise and begins anew. Either way, Godspeed, Tiger.

Self-Empowerment, Self-Leadership, and Self-Control

All life is an experiment.
The more experiments you make the better.
–Ralph Waldo Emerson

While having lunch with my life partner, best friend and wife, something occurred to me about the way my mom and my dad raised me. I shared with you in the introduction how I used to play fantasy baseball in the basement of our home for hours and hours. I'm pretty sure neither one of my parents understood what the purpose of all that was, but they never criticized me, made fun of me, or told me to spend my time doing something more productive. Their mantra always was and still is to this day that education and hard work will allow you to do whatever you want to do.

What I don't remember either one of them saying was what I couldn't do. I remember passing through a phase when I was going to buy a sailboat and sail around the world. Little things like how on earth I was going to afford this sailboat, outfit this sailboat, or even learn how to sail the sailboat were minor details that did not cloud my thoughts of sailing the seas. My memory is not precise on this one, but I think it went something like this. My mom said something to the effect of how exciting it would be to travel to so many different places and meet so many different people. I'm fairly certain my dad's advice was along the lines of learning at least one, if not two, additional foreign languages so I would be better prepared for my travels.

What I am 100 percent certain of is neither one of them told me that this was silly, not possible, or a waste of time. I am assuming they did similar things with my brothers and sisters. When you look at the Vincent family, you see a family that is highly educated and fiercely independent, and all of us are successful entrepreneurs. Just a coincidence? I think not. If you did not have a similar experience with your parents, all is not lost—in fact, nothing is lost. The beauty of life is that today is a new day. *Today* stop allowing others to tell you why your dreams are just that. *Today* stop telling others why their dreams are just that. Love, encouragement, and practical advice on how they can get to where they can go are more powerful than you may ever know.

This is a book about achieving your unique potential, so what the heck is leadership doing here? You might be thinking, "I have no desire to be a leader, so why on earth would I read this chapter?" Again, people use the words *skills* and *talents* interchangeably, but they are very different from each other. When you see the word *leadership*, you might first think about work and second about being in charge of people. First of all, leadership isn't something that only occurs at work. In fact some of the greatest leadership occurs in our neighborhoods, where we worship, and I could go on and on. Secondly, even in the context of work, leadership does not have to be about managing or supervising other people. I have had the privilege of working with some great leaders that were not particularly good at supervising anyone, especially themselves. So this begs a question: what exactly is leadership?

Wikipedia defines *leadership* as "organizing a group of people to achieve a common goal." The leader may or may not have formal authority. Students of leadership have produced theories involving traits, situational interaction, function, behavior, power, vision, values, charisma, and intelligence, among others. But basically, a leader is somebody people follow, somebody who guides or directs others.

Career-success-for-newbies.com (a very cool site, by the way) defines *leadership* this way: "a process where a leader influences the direction of a unit in achieving its objective." Cliffnotes.com describes it this way: "Common to all definitions of leadership is the notion that leaders are individuals who, by their actions, facilitate the movement of a group of people toward a common or shared goal." This definition implies that leadership is an influencing process.

So, again, what the heck is leadership doing in a book on achieving your unique potential? The answer is twofold. First that the traditional model of leaders and followers was developed during the Industrial Age. It doesn't work anymore. Treat yourself to a book entitled *Turn the Ship Around*, by David Marquet. In it he describes how, by applying a leader-leader model, they, the crew, transformed themselves, not just for the duration of his tour but for the duration of everyone's career. Secondly read all those definitions above and remember you are part of any group, you in fact are a group unto yourself. You can and need to lead you, first and foremost!

This dovetails perfectly into my belief in self-empowerment. Lots of books on leadership talk about the principle of empowering people. The problem with that is, if you have the authority to empower people, there is at least the perception that you also have the authority to disempower them. The much better and more effective approach is self-empowerment and self-leadership.

Far too many of us have fallen into victim mode. We blame them—those people. And we can't catch a break; we never can get lucky; and so on. This can turn into a lifelong rut. But those who choose the path of self-leadership and self-empowerment realize they alone are responsible for themselves and their lives. We potentially control so much more than we give ourselves credit for. We'll look at this more when we talk about nutrition and exercise, but here are some amazing facts about things that are completely within our control that wind up severely limiting or ending our lives. Are you aware that 80 percent of heart disease is preventable, as is 90 percent of type 2 diabetes? The number-one killer in America is heart disease, claiming more than six hundred thousand lives per year, and 80 percent of those deaths are preventable. Stop smoking, cut down on your drinking, get off your butt and move, lose that gut, and replace processed, fake food with vegetables and other nonprocessed foods that are as close as possible to the state they were in when they were on the tree or bush, in the ground, or swimming, flying, or walking around—and, just maybe, you won't kill yourself.

That might sound a bit brutal, but it is because I believe in the self-leadership, self-empowerment mind-set, wrapped in self control. I'm not sure who said it first, but a quote bounces in my head often: "If not me, who? If not now, when?" I freely admit that self-leadership comes easier to some people than others, but I refuse to believe that every human spirit is incapable of at least some level of self-leadership and self-empowerment. *If you are counting on anyone else other than yourself to get you to where you want to go, you will lead and live a disappointing life.*

I've talked about purpose, passion, persistence, and expertise, and now I want to mention another word that is sorely lacking in all aspects of our society: *accountability*. Accountability starts with you, and it is the spark that will lead to becoming more self-reliant, more independent, and more successful, however you define success. So how exactly does a person become a self-leader, and how exactly does he or she become self-empowered?

I have seven principles for exceptional twenty-first-century leadership. They apply equally to the boardroom and the classroom—and even the bathroom (not sure why bathroom is there but read on). Self-leadership and self-empowerment apply to all aspects of your life, if you so choose.

Here are some specific attributes of exceptional leaders:

1. Leaders are risk takers. Playing it safe gets you to OK, at best. Risk must be calculated; decision making must be thoughtful; and judgment

must be sound. In other words, you need to be right the majority of the time. But make no mistake; exceptional leaders are risk takers.

2. Leaders identify, acquire, and develop talent. The only expertise you truly need is to know who the expert is. I'm quoting myself as near as I can remember. Seek out your talents and then build skills onto them. Surround yourself will other talented people that have complementary but different talents. You can teach skill; you have to acquire talent.

3. Leaders are highly effective communicators. In *The Seven Habits of Highly Effective People*, one of the habits is "seek first to understand, then to be understood." To be truly understood, you need to know who you are communicating with. Effective communicators take the time to learn (listen) first and speak second.

4. Leaders focus first and foremost on the outcome. We still live in an activity-based world; that is why there is a morning and an evening rush hour. And it's why the deli is empty at 11:30 and the line is out the door at 12:30. In the super-fast, changing world we live in, exceptional leaders understand that looking ahead to the outcome and working back to the activities is the only effective way to stay proactive and to avoid being reactive.

5. Leaders apply consistent accountability every day. Accountability starts with you: you walk the walk, and you insist—yes, insist— that those around you do the same. Where there is no accountability, there is no hope for a healthy, positive environment.

6. Leaders never stop growing, they enjoy life. They grow not just in professional knowledge but in all of life—spiritually, emotionally, mentally, and physically. When an exceptional leader believes she has finished growing, she has in fact finished prospering. When I write, "enjoying" I mean leaders have *fun*.

7. Leaders do everything they can to ensure others do first six things as well. Another way to say this is *exceptional leaders develop exceptional leaders*.

Lead yourself if you have no interest in others leading you. When you do, by example you will be leading others. Pretty cool, actually.

I have given you tools for creating goals. There is a chapter that includes why we resist change, (WOW, is this powerful) and how to overcome it. I have written about how to be more effective in communication. I have discussed what makes us unique and why that is our competitive advantage in achieving our unique potential. And in almost every chapter, there is some mention of looking at the result: where you want to wind up, the outcome.

If you are in a bad relationship, I encourage you to envision what a good relationship —a wonderful relationship, a perfect relationship— looks like or feels like or smells like. Then be a leader and talk with your partner, asking first how he or she feels about the relationship. Then encourage him or her to share with you a vision of a different future. Remember, if you want to be understood, you have to seek to understand. Be willing to listen and be willing to change if you want to make the relationship work.

I have had my failures in relationships, but I have found a magnificent relationship now, and I can attest that a healthy, loving, growing relationship is possible using all the guiding principles listed above. It involves risk to have the hard conversations, and it takes effective communication skills to ensure that hard conversations are effective. It takes consistent accountability, starting with you, and an understanding of your talents and strengths and your partner's as well to avoid frustrations in the day-to-day tasks of living. Focus on a healthy purpose and outcome for the relationship and on a willingness to keep growing so that the relationship stays vibrant. Finally, you need to be willing to encourage your partner to do all of the same.

As is the case with most things in my life, I've only come to understand the power of self-empowerment and self-leadership during the past ten years. Sobriety is impossible without accountability, self-leadership, and self-empowerment. If you reach a point where you feel a relationship cannot fulfill your needs, then applying, accountability, self-leadership, and self-empowerment is the only path to a brighter tomorrow.

Even though it is important to seek to understand and then be understood, it is a mistake not to be prepared to discuss what is important to you. I have not always been successful in correcting a poor relationship, but I now understand how to work through the bumps in the road. Now I am in the most wonderful, caring, transparent, and beautiful relationship anyone could ever be blessed with. It took a tremendous amount of accountability to correct unacceptable behaviors on my part, and then self-leadership and self-empowerment. Two critical points here I want to drive home. First, remember, *if you want to see change in others, you need to change first*. The second point is sometimes relationships fail, for any number of reasons, they fail. "Sticking it out" for whatever reason is always going to adversely affect both of you, forever. Sometimes the best thing to do for both partners is to move on.

As is the case with everything in this book, this applies to your career too. I've given examples of self-control, self-leadership, and self-empowerment. Every time you decide you're going to do something despite people telling you all the reasons you can't, you are holding yourself accountable and you are exercising self-empowerment. It works at home, it works at work, it works. Remember, you have one life. Live it! Self-empowerment and leadership help in another area: procrastination. Yikes.

I was visiting my son in Charleston, South Carolina, and we went out to Folly Beach, which is largely undisturbed by commercial development. As we were leaving the beach, we saw on a corner, a little bar. It was the kind of place I would've spent a great deal of time in back in my drinking days. This bar had a bright neon sign in the window. I had been by tens of thousands of bars in and walked into a majority of them, so I have seen tens of thousands of neon bar signs. But I had never seen this one. It said, "free beer tomorrow."

How absolutely brilliant in its simplicity! From the point of view of the proprietor, it tells patrons to come back tomorrow for free beer. Of course when they come back tomorrow, the sign still says, "free beer tomorrow."

So many of us will never achieve our unique potential for one simple yet extremely powerful reason: we're waiting for tomorrow.

- "I'm going to go back to school as soon as the children are a little older."
- "I'm going to talk to my boss about moving up in the organization in another year or so, when I've gained more experience."
- "As soon as things calm down at work, I'm going to go to the local community college and take those Spanish classes."
- "When Bob and I retire from the school district, we're going to take that trip to Europe."
- "My New Year's resolution for the upcoming year is going to be to lose twenty pounds and get back in that beautiful suit before my reunion."

On and on it goes. It's like when your transmission goes out in your car, and you say, "Not now. Why did the transmission have to die now?" As if there is a good time for your transmission to go out. You have one life; there are always going to be valid reasons for you to wait to start what you feel is important or needed to improve your life or to provide happiness. There will always be valid reasons not to start today. So guess what; you're going to do it tomorrow.

But just like free beer tomorrow, tomorrow never comes. So don't get an idea or two out of this book and say, "Wow, I think I'm going to do _____ next week, next month, next year." *Take action immediately.* We don't know what tomorrow will bring, and the list of reasons not to start today might include even more significant reasons tomorrow. So, although this section started with "free beer tomorrow," I'm going to spend the rest of the chapter writing about taking action today to live a better life, a healthier life, and a more fulfilling life.

When I talk about skill, I'm talking about skill being made up of knowledge and experience. When I talk about wellness, I'm talking about nutrition, spirituality, emotions, and physical fitness. People are somewhat surprised that the Genesis Group, a company with expertise in maximizing human capital, holds wellness as one of its cornerstones. We believe it would be irresponsible for us to talk about maximizing human capital without discussing wellness.

Self-leadership, self control and self-empowerment also are critical to living a healthy financial life, something I FAILED to do for much of my adult life, but NOW I understand and am living this AMAZINGLY powerful method:

Living Below Your Means
A man (or woman) in debt is so far a slave.
Ralph Waldo Emerson

Again, if you have not read Dave Ramsey's *Total Money Makeover* or *The Millionaire Next Door*, written by Thomas Stanley and William Danko immediately purchase both (pay cash or with a debit card, please, no credit) and read them at least twice. Everything I have talked about in this book and everything I have offered as tools for you to achieve your unique potential won't matter much if you don't have two nickels in your pocket.

I write, "Live below your means," though the more conventional phrase is "Live within your means." Most of us can't even define "within our means," and many unfortunately live well beyond our means. It took divorce for me to examine the way I looked at spending money and savings. I think back to those days in the navy when we just sat around and waited for payday; we absolutely lived paycheck to paycheck. We would spend 80 percent of our paycheck within two or three days, knowing it was twelve more days before we got paid again. Do you live that way?

Unfortunately and embarrassingly, the household I was part of continued that spending pattern even when my income went up significantly. I was making more money than I ever could have imagined in advertising sales, but we were still living paycheck to paycheck. This is particularly challenging when your income is 100 percent commission. You don't know how much your next paycheck is going to be. It was a recipe for disaster that was fully baked.

I am not a financial expert. I offer no financial advice other than this: read the two books I recommended and live a cash life. I have seen so many examples of insanity when it comes to finances, that my head is clear on the topic. I am not going to be a hypocrite, because many of these things I have done myself, but I am going to tell you that I have become reborn, if you will. The following are my interpretations of what I learned from those two great books I recommended at the beginning of this section. They may be different than what is written in their books because these are the things I have found work best for me.

Figure out how much cash you need to live for three months. When I say "live," I mean all bills, food, gas, clothing, and other essentials—no luxury items, no additional purchases, not even new clothes, providing the clothes you have are serviceable. Scrimp and save first before you do anything else—up to and including paying the minimum on whatever you owe until you have this four-month emergency fund to cover your essential living in place. Transmissions go bad; dental bills are not covered by insurance—life brings us many unexpected financial challenges. Catastrophic medical challenges are completely beyond our control, but the smaller unforeseen occurrences actually can be seen, and they can be prepared for.

Live below your means; don't spend everything you make and then some. Before you do anything else, before you pay a bill off, before you pay down more than what the required minimum is so you can stay current, build up that four-month reserve. When life throws its unexpected expenditures at you, the money for it comes out of your cushion. Then immediately stop paying extra or saving for a car or saving for whatever you might need, and go back to putting money away until you have that four-month reserve.

Here are some amazing things that I bet you didn't know about millionaires. I know I didn't know them until I read *The Millionaire Next Door*, by Thomas Stanley and William Danko.

- The average millionaire lives in a house worth $320,000.
- Eighty percent did not inherit their wealth.

- Only a small percentage paid more than $399 for a suit. Less than 10 percent have ever spent more than a thousand dollars on a piece of jewelry. And a minority drive a current model year automobile.
- Eighty percent are college graduates; only 30 percent have advanced degrees.
- On average, they invested nearly 20 percent of their household income each year.
- Only 50 percent of millionaires have ever spent more than $235 for a wristwatch.
- Only 50 percent have ever spent more than $140 on a pair of shoes

Now, you may be wondering who the heck would ever spend $140 on a pair of shoes. Or who the heck has $235 to spend on a wristwatch. But think about it. According to *The Millionaire Next Door*, the average millionaire's total annualized realized income is $131,000. Now, that is a great deal of money, but how many people own a home that's less than three times their household income in value? Another way to ask this question is, if you had a taxable income of $131,000, would you spend more than $235 on a wristwatch or $140 on a pair of shoes? I believe if you're being honest, many would say yes. Well before I made the income I make now, I spent significantly more on both shoes and wristwatches than the average millionaire. I overspent.

If you don't have cash, don't buy it.

Dave Ramsey is proud to say that he actually has no credit score. He pays cash for everything, up to and including houses. Now, this obviously is an extreme example, but his point is well taken. Ramsey says to save until you can afford to pay cash for a $1,500 car. The money you save on a car payment you can probably put in the bank—or keep under your mattress, since a mattress pays about the same rate as a bank these days. If you follow the advice of his book, your life will improve, you will likely have more income, and you will likely have a better state of mind to allocate that income. So perhaps you save $4,000. You get rid of that $1,500 car for $750, and you buy a new car for $4,750, and so on.

If you don't have the cash, don't buy it.

WOW, Is This Powerful!

For every minute you remain angry,
you give up sixty seconds of peace of mind.
—Ralph Waldo Emerson

Time doesn't heal wounds,
what you do with time is what heals wounds.
—Kathy Selby

I wonder how many of you saw the title of this chapter in the table of contents and immediately turned to it. If you haven't read anything else in the book, yet, I recommend you read this chapter. The theme of the entire book is that we all learn differently, live differently, think differently, communicate differently, and so on. And I'm hopeful that once this is learned, however you learned it, it is applied, however you apply it. You need to learn and then apply what you learn if you want to improve and to achieve your unique potential in life. That is universal: applying what you learn is the "git r done" part of the learning process.

Often we learn in a trial by fire. In other words, we learn and gain experience because we are thrown into a situation and are essentially told, "Good luck and God bless." If we do actually learn and we do actually survive long enough to gain experience, we have added skill. When talent is added to this mix, if the talent is significant enough and the skill becomes significant enough, we have strength. Operate in your strengths long enough, and the strength becomes expertise. Our expertise is what separates us from everyone else.

In keeping with the ramblings in many other parts of the book, this chapter is not about skills and talents; it is about the most powerful formula that applies directly to achieving your potential.

At the beginning of this book I promised to provide practical tools you can adapt to your particular style and apply. And when it comes to tools, simple beats complicated. And practical beats theoretical. So here's the formula that is a complete game changer:

$$EVENT + REACTION = OUTCOME$$

I think I first saw this in Jack Canfield's *Chicken Soup for the Soul.* Again, I read fifty or sixty books a year. Actually, I skim them, grabbing the key points, then applying them to my life. I learn and apply what I have learned, as I go, generally forgetting where things came from. So, if the "event plus reaction equals outcome" formula was originally spoken by someone else or not spoken or written at all by Jack Canfield, I apologize.

When I first saw the formula and began to think about it, I fundamentally agreed with it. My experience and my focus for most of my adult life have been to try to control the event and minimize the negative effects of my reactions, and those two would produce an outcome. If you've skipped around this book, you've probably found out that one of the things I love is leadership. Some people call leading being in charge, but my definition of leadership is not at all related to being in charge of other people. It is related to improving people's lives, improving organizations, and improving situations through your spirit, your expertise, your will, and your example. *It is about teaching people about leading themselves.*

As I wrote in the preceding paragraph, I spent the majority of my time and energy trying to control events instead of working on my reactions to them. My reactions really were more of an afterthought. This was particularly important during my active drinking years. If you have struggled with or are struggling with addiction, you know that your life is centered on two things: one, preventing anything from getting in the way of your drug of choice, and two, refuting anyone who says you have a problem. For me, it meant controlling events as much as possible so those events had a minimum impact on my ability to get to a barstool or the vodka in my drawer.

Somewhat related to my alcoholism was an extremely volatile temper. Although I'm now a complete subscriber to one life, my temper rarely displayed itself outside work, and when it did it was not at the level it was a work. People that knew me, particularly in the military, were very familiar with my flash temper. I was Mr. Happy-Go-Lucky as long as the events were going as I wanted them to go. When they did not, my reaction was horrific. So when I originally looked at this formula, my thoughts turned to how correct it was, but I didn't really understand the significance of it. Only after I allowed my reaction to certain events to change the event itself did I begin to realize that this formula was not a fifty-fifty formula. I realized very quickly that *the event itself was not nearly as critical to the outcome as my reaction to the event*. This was true on several levels.

Early in my years of supervision, I experienced one of the most powerful and embarrassing examples of what happens when you let your reaction overshadow the event. I was a leading petty officer on a submarine. A leading petty officer is simply the senior enlisted person in charge of the division, sometimes below a chief petty officer. In this case I was also the senior person in the division. I had a junior enlisted who was responsible for creating tide and current graphs for an upcoming underway (when a ship, or in my case a submarine, leaves the pier for the open sea).

Tides and currents are very important for any ship navigating in and out of a port, since they affect how the ship or submarine steers. When the tide is coming in, it is called a flood tide. When the tide is going out, it is called an ebb tide. In some rivers, these currents move very quickly. The faster the current, the more effect it has on the submarine; it determines what type of corrections need to be made to ensure the submarine turns in the proper spot and stays in the safe and navigable waters.

This is not a complicated calculation; however, the junior petty officer brought me a completed tides and currents report that simply made no sense. The times he had listed for when the maximum flood current would be running were three hours different from what the graph showed. I was not sure which was correct—or which was incorrect—but I knew either the times or the graph was wrong.

I sent the petty officer away and told him to check his work and to correct it. I could feel the anger building inside of me, knowing what was going to happen. Sure enough, the young man came back less than an hour later and said that he had found the problem and corrected it. But once again the times did not make sense based on what the graph revealed. I became absolutely furious. After a childish bout of yelling and screaming at the young man, I abruptly walked away and returned several minutes later. I will skip the details of what I did next. Suffice it to say my reaction to what was a relatively minor error, caught long before it caused any issues, was completely inappropriate (let your mind wander here, *really inappropriate*). Essentially this reaction, my reaction, caused a completely new event and a very different outcome. My out-of-control, immature, and frankly dangerous reaction to the event changed the event and created a new set of potential outcomes.

Later I apologized profusely and told the young man I did not mean anything that I said or anything that I did; but the damage was done. I immediately broke into a meeting with the navigator, who was my boss, and the ship's executive officer, second in charge to the commanding officer. I told them what I had just done, essentially placing myself on report. Some administrative action was taken, some paperwork was signed, and a letter was placed in my record.

But here is the purpose of this story as it relates to the EVENT + REACTION = OUTCOME formula. The event was a tide and current graph being done incorrectly. In the overall scope of things, as long as the mistake was caught and corrected, which it was, this event would not have been a big deal. My reaction to the event was so unprofessional and unacceptable that it not only changed the outcome, it replaced the original event as the focus with a new event, my reaction, leading to a whole new direction.

We do not learn nearly as much when we get things right as we do when we get things wrong. Mistakes are the greatest teacher we could possibly have. Although I'm ashamed of this specific mistake, it served as a powerful turning point in how I viewed both events and my reactions to events. It would not be truthful to say I completely eliminated my temper after that day; I did not. But never again did I allow my reaction to an event create a more significant, "replacement" event.

Let's look at events and reactions. If you use this book as the practical handbook to reach your unique potential, the road to that potential will not be without issues, challenges, and setbacks. When you live your life, bad or unexpected things happen. These are "events"—illness, injury, downsizing, terrible neighbors, lousy in-laws, deteriorating personal relationships, horrible bosses and/or peers. The list of events that can affect our lives is endless. And many, if not most, of them are partially or completely outside our control. I'm using negative events here, because they tend to hold attention and drill deeper than positive events but this formula applies equally to positive or negative events.

So, as discussed in the chapter that discusses time management (chapter 3), seek first to be effective, then to be efficient. It makes no sense to spend your time and energy trying to control something you can never control. I am not suggesting you ignore the events or ignore mistakes that come out of events. We can learn and we can grow, and mistakes are a wonderful learning tool as long as they are measured and as long as they are not repeated. My point is that you have zero chance of controlling all the events that will affect you.

The *great news* is that your reaction is 100 percent controlled by you. Yet we rarely, if ever, spend our emotional intelligence, our skills, and our talents in reacting better to an event. If we learn to control our reaction regardless of what happens with the event, we have a positive impact on the outcome. Let's examine more closely why we react and how we react.

I wrote earlier about how little we are able to process in our conscious mind. At the most, we can process five, six, maybe seven lines of active thought. Our subconscious mind has the ability to process millions of bits of data in a second. The best way for you to understand how much influence your subconscious has in your reaction is another example. Soon after moving into a new neighborhood, a person came and proceeded to ask me extremely in-depth personal questions about who I was, why I was there, where I was from, what I did, why I did it. To put it mildly, this person was very invasive and uncomfortably intrusive.

From that day forward, if I was out working in the yard and I saw him peering over the hedge, almost like Wilson from the TV show *Tool Time*, it was fight or flight time. My stomach balled up and I realized the Spanish Inquisition was moments away. I pretended to be on my Bluetooth; I walked around the other side of the house; I did anything to avoid this person. He was the event, and my reaction was based on the fact that he really made me uncomfortable.

This is where the subconscious comes into play. He does not nor did he ever make me uncomfortable. It is not possible for another human being to evoke an emotion from within you. You create the emotion. You create the feeling. One of the programs we offer at the Genesis Group is "They don't drive you crazy, YOU drive you crazy." The science and the facts behind this are simple. That neighbor provided a bad first experience, and he quickly was filed in my subconscious with other similar unpleasant experiences with people. So when I saw or heard the neighbor, my subconscious grabbed and brought to my conscious mind past experiences so quickly it made me feel as if that person was causing the emotion. I felt and "knew" he was causing my reaction. In fact, I was causing the reaction.

I would like to tell you I had a straightforward conversation with him, telling him that I found him to be intrusive and troubling and that I no longer wished to speak with him. I would like to tell you that is how I handled it, but I did not. By nature I prefer to avoid confrontation. That being said, when it is necessary, I do it, and I am actually very good at it, but it is not my preference.

So how did I react to this event to get to the outcome I desired (not talking with this creepy old guy)? I put my Bluetooth earpiece in, whether I was using it or not, whether my phone was even with me or even turned on. Every time that man began advancing, I pointed to the ear piece. Now, I never said out loud I was on a call, but he'd apparently equated my hand gesture to that and would somewhat sheepishly withdraw. Feel free to use that one.

The real takeaway here is that *you* are creating the feeling of angst, nervousness, or nausea, not another person. The exception would be if you're breathing foul air or being affected by other environmental causes. But I assure you that people are not creating those feelings in you; you are. This is true every time; this is true without exception.

Don't let people live rent free in your head.
Alcoholics Anonymous

As powerful as this thought is, real power comes only with being able to control it. To control it, we have to dig a little deeper. Our reactions are a combination of three things: feelings, thought, and action. Personality styles and Dr. Carl Jung teach us that some people are very-strong-feelings people while others are more nonemotional in their approach. However, everybody feels first. When one of the five senses sends something to your brain, it first passes through the limbic system. This is the first stop along the way to thought and action in the brain. In other words, all of us are wired the same way. The difference between feelings people and those who approach things with less emotion is simply how much weight we put on our feelings; but all of us feel first. The majority of us then think with varying degrees of feeling attached to that thought. Then an action—or what I'm calling a reaction— occurs. So a reaction to an event is the sum of our feelings, our thoughts, and the actions we decide to take based on our feelings and our thoughts. Keep in mind that our feelings and our thoughts are heavily affected by our subconscious mind, specifically our historical data stored in there.

So why does all this matter? Because once we understand the power of our subconscious and once we understand the flow of how our mind processes information, we are in a very powerful position. In this position we can change our reaction; we can control our reaction. When we force ourselves into a conscious decision to react differently from what our instincts are, we are reprogramming our subconscious mind.

A very practical example of this would be how we react when we get stuck in traffic. Let's set the stage with us getting a late start and heading to pick our child up from soccer practice. Halfway there, we come across an accident, and the traffic comes to a complete stop. We now have visions of our eight-year-old being left on the field by himself—the sun setting and him horribly alone and afraid. Feelings, thoughts, all sorts of things occur. We grow fearful, and anxiety and panic set in. We might lean on the horn, slap the steering wheel, turn up the music to drown our thoughts, or even scream in the silence of our car. Of course, none of this does anything to change the event.

We might initially have feelings of anxiety, fear, anger, or a combination thereof, but if we react out of anger and fear, we won't have the best reaction to the event. If we force ourselves into our conscious mind, we can work through the feelings, and then we can think of what the best reaction is for that specific event. So our feelings lead to our thoughts, and our thoughts lead to the action we take, which leads to our reaction.

In this scenario, instead of wasting time scrambling, yelling, or trying to find back roads, we force ourselves to consciousness and become more rational. In doing this, we have better control over our thoughts and our feelings, and we are almost certainly going to come up with a better action plan. Let's call one of the other parents and see if she can pick up our child. Now you might say, "Gee, no kidding," but would you really get there as quickly if you were in the moment? Most of us would waste time with emotion and with actions that have nothing to do with producing the best outcome.

When we learn to control our reaction better, we are also reprogramming our subconscious. The more consistent we are with this, the less effort it takes to react better to similar events. This is simply because we will be reprogramming our own unconscious mind, and when we run across similar events in the future, our "databank" in our subconscious will be filled with better reactions.

Before moving on, here's a serious word of caution. Do not leave this section thinking reacting emotionally is bad. Controlled, appropriate use of emotions can be powerful, not hurtful. Women specifically are often told to keep their emotions in check in business. I am not a woman but I am an extremely effective communicator and negotiator. A key to my success is my effective use of emotion. I also have witnessed firsthand highly successful businesswoman use controlled emotion to their advantage. This book uses the word *passion* frequently. If you think emotion is a bad thing, change it out for passion. When you react to an event, are you reacting emotionally or are you reacting with passion? Hmm.

But wait, there's more. **HOW COOL IS THIS:**

Always do what you are afraid to do.
Ralph Waldo Emerson

No, not just the quote, but all the stuff that follows, silly. If you are really going to benefit from the nuggets presented in this book you are going to have to apply them. Applying them means you are going to have to change and change scares 99% of us. What follows is a more powerful thought specifically on the subject of effectively managing change.

It was a warm, sunny day in May in Pensacola, Florida, when I retired from the navy. My last assignment had been as a command master chief of a large training command. I was responsible for five detachments around the country; a total of a few thousand sailors, airmen, soldiers, coast guardsmen, and marines were passing through the doors of our classrooms. I was the senior enlisted person in the entire operation, with a nice corner office with leather furniture, an extremely capable and dedicated executive administrator, and operational authority over a significant number of senior enlisted personnel around the country.

Command master chiefs don't need appointments to see the commanding officer, or anyone else, for that matter. There's an unspoken fact in all branches of service about the senior enlisted pay grade, known as E-9. The truth is, you are as high as you can go. So, yes, there are people with aspirations of moving up the command master chief or the command sergeant major food chain, to more senior roles, but for most, you are at the pinnacle of your career. Unless you kill somebody, there really isn't much anybody can do to you, discipline wise and, frankly, career wise, either, because the reality is you are as senior as you can go. To be factually correct, other than not recommending you for reenlistment, which would mean you would have to retire at the end of your present enlistment, there really is pretty much nothing anybody can do to you. I won't say that this is abused by those in the senior enlisted pay grade, but they certainly are aware of it, as is everyone else.

At my retirement ceremony at the Naval Air Museum at Naval Air Station Pensacola, somewhere in the neighborhood of fifteen hundred people filled the place up to the rafters. It was a big deal, and I was the center of the big deal. I was wrapping up an extremely successful twenty-year career. Even though the pay was not great, it was steady. Every two weeks for twenty years I had gotten a check. As long as I was breathing and didn't do anything really stupid, I was getting paid. So there I was, top of the food chain, king of the hill, big deal, big-time job, and steady pay unaffected by economic conditions or pretty much anything else going on in the world. Overall, it was a pretty good gig.

In an hour it was over.

Three days later I reported to work as an account executive at a CBS television affiliate station. I was at the complete bottom of the sales food chain. My steady paycheck was replaced by no paycheck whatsoever. I was a salesperson on 100 percent commission. In other words, I sell or I don't eat. My corner office with the leather furniture overlooking the base—in our case the old airfield—was replaced by a tiny office, in a strip mall, with a few pieces of mismatched furniture and no windows.

Instead of being responsible for a few thousand people, I instantly was responsible for finding a few thousand dollars of advertising revenue a week. On Friday I could've made a phone call and pretty much made anything happen in my considerable universe. On Monday morning I was that "new guy" salesperson who didn't know his own phone number, where his desk was, what his job was, or much of anything else. I went from near the pinnacle of the enlisted ranks in the US Navy to a complete nobody by just about any definition of the word.

Now, that is what I call a life-changing event, and it happened over the course of a weekend, start to finish.

The majority of us never achieve our unique potential, never achieve whatever we define success as, because *we do not take the action necessary to change.* I have talked openly in this book of my challenge with mental illness and my challenge with alcohol. I failed in marriage my first time around, and I have made more mistakes than I can count in virtually every area of life. Heck, if I was so messed up, why on earth would you be taking your precious time to read this book? Great question! My answer is *I was* not *I am.* I am not holding myself up in this book as some hero who has overcome insurmountable odds; frankly, I think my story is typical. Certainly many people have done more with less and overcome significantly more. I do know many people that do not appear to have more baggage but always have a reason *not* to change. They fall victim to themselves and their innate fear of change.

No matter who you are, no matter what you come up against, you can do more if you want to.

This is a great quote for you to read over and over again. Making mistakes does not lead to failure; not correcting mistakes or not taking action in the first place does. Here's another way to say something similar: the only way to guarantee you never make a mistake is to never make a decision, that leads to action, which is the greatest mistake of all.

If you commit to achieving your unique potential and the success that comes from that, there are two universal truths: you must take responsible and calculated risk, and you must overcome your fear of change. Because we are all unique, everyone gets there differently, but I absolutely assure you, without hesitation, that without risk taking and without overcoming fear of change, you will be paralyzed with indecision, second guessing, and procrastination.

I thought it would be helpful to explain, as I did in other sections about the conscious and subconscious and about how our reactions occur, to delve into what I call the change cycle. I did not create this diagram; I've seen it in various forms in various books and online. This version is customized to drive some key points.

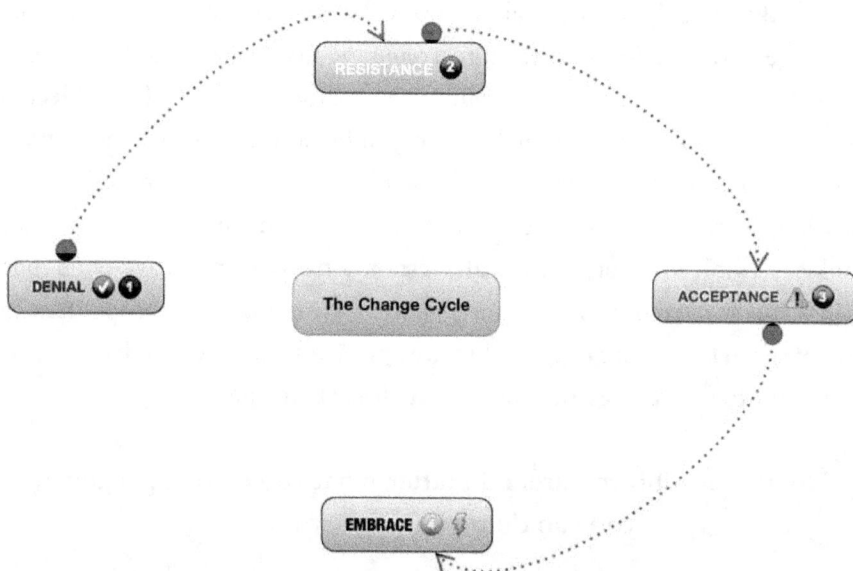

The first phase that every human being goes through when facing change is denial. Make no mistake; even the most change-embracing human goes through denial. For all those reasons that make us unique, he might do it extremely quickly—so fast that he doesn't even think he's considering it, feeling it, or thinking about it. But I assure you that when it comes to significant change, everybody goes through denial. Many of us never get past this; we stay in denial, almost guaranteeing change either will not occur or will not occur in a positive way.

After moving through denial, the next stop on the tour is resistance. Resistance happens when the pressure to change your life, your career, your work habits, or your relationships becomes so great you have to do something to show that you're moving in the direction. We don't like this. It doesn't feel good, and we likely drag our feet. If the personal pressure or the outside pressure is great enough, though, we move through resistance and get to acceptance.

Please note that *acceptance* does not mean agreement. Alcoholics Anonymous and other addiction programs teach this. What acceptance does mean is compliance. What acceptance does mean is "I understand and I will accept." If there is action associated with the change, a person who accepts that change is now operating fully in compliance with the change. Again, it matters not if the change is related to your work or your personal life; only with acceptance can you move on.

Someone has a serious illness or suffers a serious injury or loses their job, the *longer* she spends in the "why me?" phase, the more she hurts herself. The much more powerful question is, "What now?" A dear friend who died way too young used to tell me all the time when I was lamenting something, "It is what it is." I initially really resented that expression but now I have a wooden sign in my office with those words on it. That phrase does not mean you have no control or no free will. In fact, it is just the opposite. It is the ultimate setup for EVENT + REACTION. "It is what it is" is the event.

I think you might agree that we do not control most events; they are what they are. But you have control and free will to shape your reaction. Here's another similar expression: "Wherever you go, there you are." Think about it, please. Things happen to us because they do. Mistakes happen because they do. Tragedies occur because tragedies occur. Those that recover are those that move forward; those that continue to *live* the best life possible are those that stop saying "why me?" and start saying "what's next?"

You will notice in the diagram a little alert sign next to acceptance. You will also notice that *embrace* is in bold. There are two reasons for these. If you are a supervisor and you are leading change, your responsibility is to, as quickly and as effectively as possible, get those people you are supervising and managing to the acceptance part of change. Whether they ever embrace it is a personal journey. That being said, those that are going to get the most out of this book and those that are going to achieve their unique potential will face the necessary change, take the necessary risks, and embrace the change that moves them toward their goals. Only through embracing can you experience the passion necessary to fuel you for future change and for future growth opportunities. Remember that passion is the fuel that drives persistence and leads to achieving your purpose. Also notice it is the change circle, not the change line. It is a circle because in order to achieve our unique potential in life we must continue the improvement the growth and the change throughout our lives.

The second part of this chapter deals with risk taking. The only way to ensure you never make a mistake is to never make a decision. Not making a decision is the biggest mistake of all. I was walking through one of my favorite stores in the world not too long ago—Barnes & Noble. I saw out of the corner of my eye a book entitled *Thank You for Firing Me.* I didn't need to pick up the book to know what its premise was. I have fired myself twice (a next level of "thank you for firing me").

When the navy no longer fit my purpose and no longer provided the challenges that created my passion, I lost persistence and lost interest, and I fired myself. And after five years in the world of outside advertising sales, I had to have a very difficult conversation with myself in the mirror. During that conversation, I fired myself. Again, the reasons were the same: the job was not meeting my purpose in life. I had lost my passion, so I had to go— and I truly mean, *had* to go.

Most people do not fire themselves; they leave a job for another job, and that is absolutely logical and reasonable. If you get laid off, you get fired, or your position is eliminated, what then? What happens when you lose your job without another? This is when many people take that leap into a completely new field they always wanted to be in. These events typically allow us to skip right past denial and resistance and jump into acceptance. Risk taking never enters into our mind in this scenario because we better do something, now! This is when the hobby becomes the job, and you start your own business. Is there risk? You bet. But here's a universal truth: almost everything worth having, almost anything that defines success, has risk involved. There are countless stories of people that lose their jobs, walk away from their jobs, or wake up one morning and decide they're not going to live an unhealthy life anymore. Sometimes this decision is caused by the illness or death of a loved one. Sometimes it is caused by a wake-up call, such as a heart attack or the discovery of another medical problem related to an unhealthy lifestyle.

My point is this: sometimes the risk to fundamentally change our lives is caused by outside influences. These outside influences sometimes shock us right through the first two steps of the change cycle into acceptance and then action to do something differently. Personality has a huge amount to do with how much risk we are willing to take. There are also other factors, such as generational differences, cultural differences, our financial and family situations—and the list goes on and on.

No two people are ever in the exact same situation, so there are no guidelines for risk taking other than this: whatever risk level you are comfortable with, move it up a notch or two. You do not want to be irresponsible with the level of risk you take, but life rewards risk takers.

Life rewards those that take action while others wait. There is also a direct correlation between risk taking and a person's ability to recover from setbacks.

Also, when you have the courage to push the envelope a bit and try something that falls into the calculated risk category, and it does not work out, you did not fail. You simply had a setback. Thomas Edison was asked if he ever felt bad about failing a hundred times in the invention of the light bulb. He stated he didn't fail a hundred times; he simply figured out a hundred ways not to make a light bulb. Steve Jobs was actually fired from Apple before clawing his way back in, and the rest is history. Much to the disappointment of his parents, Michael Dell dropped out of college and started a little computer company that became Dell Computers. Tony Robbins was a janitor when he decided he had a message to share with people. Richard Simmons was morbidly obese when he woke up one day sick and tired and decided to regain his health. I am sharing business stories here because personal stories are much harder to come by. But I don't mind sharing mine.

In the fall of 2001, I was sitting on a bar stool having too much to drink. The bartender, who was someone I worked with in the navy, asked me a simple question: "Do you think you have a problem with alcohol?" I quickly and emphatically said, "Absolutely not." I went on to say I had never been in a car accident, never gotten a DUI, never beaten my wife or children, never been fired from a job because of my drinking, so no, I did not have a problem. Without hesitation she said, "That makes sense. You should wait until you kill that family of four from Ohio one night while driving drunk; then you will have a problem." She went about her business serving, and I went about my business drinking.

But her words would not leave my head twenty-four hours a day, seven days a week, for about ten days. All I could hear was her comment about not having a problem until I kill that family of four. This is where risk taking meets change. I stopped drinking in November of 2001, but I was not living a sober life. I went on a very bad three- or four-day binge in November of 2002.

November 23, 2002, is the day my life started over. It was my first day dedicated to sobriety. I embraced change and moved out of denial. Although there was a fair amount of career risk involved, given my seniority and fast accent, I went public with my alcoholism. With the help and guidance of a bunch of amazing people in a nasty upstairs room over a furniture store I embraced the AA twelve-step program and it moved me through the change cycle. Out of denial after nearly thirty *years* of it, I quickly moved into resistance. And I spent a good deal of time there. To reiterate an earlier comment there was a good deal of risk in tackling my alcoholism at that point of my career. To fully embrace my sobriety, I had to have some very open, tough conversations with a lot of people. Some of those conversations were potentially damaging to what was an extremely bright future in the navy.

I pushed through that to acceptance, and for the next two years ground it out, hoping I would wake up one day without the thirst. Turns out I wound up embracing sobriety in stages, and the thirst was not gone when I did it. Again, this is where risk met change in a very personal way, and it was the beginning of a journey that continues today. And with God's help and guidance, coupled with a healthy grip on my free will, it will continue for the rest of my life.

That lady who I credit with planting the seed of sobriety in my soul died suddenly of a brain aneurysm in May of 2011. She was in her late forties. Not only did she cause me to have to look deep inside myself and was the spark for me to deal with my alcoholism, but also in death she reminded me in a very personal and fundamental way that tomorrow is promised to no one, *so do it today, my friend.*

I want to say one more thing about my battle and the blessing that is sobriety. There is a chapter in this book entitled "Take Three *P*s and Call Me in the Morning." Those three *P*s—passion, persistence, purpose—come into play in everything we do that is worth doing. My purpose was to become clean and sober. It began with a belief and a passion provided by strangers in AA meetings long before I had any belief or any faith or any passion of my own. But I had to have passion in some form because, whether your struggle is for two years or thirty, if you do not have unwavering persistence to get to that purpose, you will not succeed. Again, passion is the fuel for persistence to get you to your purpose.

LIVE a Healthy LIFE...PLEASE!

Throw Your Diet Out with the Chips and Dip

The first wealth is health.
—Ralph Waldo Emerson

There is more misinformation in the worlds of fitness and nutrition than the combined rhetoric of the Democratic and Republican parties. For anyone that pays even the smallest amount of attention to politics, that's saying something.

But before I say another word about nutrition, fitness, or their combined result—wellness—I make the following disclaimer required both by common sense and by my legal adviser: before beginning any type of exercise or nutrition program, consult your physician. I am not a doctor, credentialed nutritionist, or formally qualified in anything I am about to share with you. The obvious question is, why on earth bother to read it then? The answer to the obvious question is because I am a personal example of the level of wellness that can be achieved without insane workout programs or "diets" that eat plenty of your money but do not produce lasting results. Furthermore, dozens and dozens of people who have followed my simple advice, after talking with their physicians, have seen similar results.

I am at the same level of health, activity, and youthfulness as I was the day I entered the navy as a super-fit guy in 1983. The difference is I'm thirty pounds heavier now, with the majority of that being muscle. In 1983 I had a thirty-eight-inch chest, and my pants were 30x32. Today I have a fourth-three-inch chest, and my pants are 32x32. Nothing else has changed: not blood pressure, not cholesterol, not my cardio fitness level, even my body fat % has only moved up 3%—essentially, no "getting older" stuff at all.

Let me start with a bit of history. I was the ultimate dichotomy. An alcoholic who smoked two packs of cigarettes a day for many years. At the same time I was eating well, led a very active life, and exercised faithfully. Many people not familiar with the military think the exercise portion is mandatory. I can assure you that for all but the last three or four years I spent on submarines, exercise and fitness enforcement came in the form of a wink. I believe my eating habits and exercise habits went a long way to offset the damaging behavior of alcoholism and chain smoking. I say that because I emerged on the other side with no damage at all related to the drinking and no sign of damage to my lungs.

I got more active after I retired from the navy. At the encouragement of a good friend in Pensacola, Florida, I discovered and became addicted to mountain biking. I continued to try to eat fairly well for the most part, and with my increased level of exercise, I arguably was in the best shape of my life in the first part of 2005. Then came my acceptance of an offer to become a sales manager, which meant a move. Over the next three years, I stopped all physical exercise. I also stopped eating decent food, relegating myself to chips, hot dogs, and anything else I could catch on the run. In early 2005, the waist size on my pants was a 32. My weight in early 2005 was 175 pounds.

But weight is a terrible measure of progress. Due mostly to water weight but some other factors as well, a 175-pound man can fluctuate in weight by as much as four pounds in a single day. It's even worse for women. Actually, a ninety-nine-cent cloth tape measure is the simplest, cheapest, and most accurate way to track a changing physical form.

But I digress. Three years later, I was stuffing myself into a pair of 36-waist pants. My belly measurement had ballooned to forty-three inches; I had added nine inches of fat around my waist in three years. My cholesterol had nearly doubled; my resting pulse had gone from the low seventies to just under a hundred beats per minute. My blood pressure had gone from 110/70 to 170/105. I was tired all the time, cranky more often than not, and generally miserable. It is said that most alcoholics have to hit bottom before they find the strength to do something about their disease. For me, understanding the profound negative effect wellness—or in my case, lack of wellness—had on every aspect of my life was an awakening as powerful as anything I had ever experienced.

I had decided to fire myself from my position in the advertising world and start my own company. I knew the overwhelming odds were against my startup surviving and reaching profitability. I became absolutely convinced that my fate would be sealed if I did not regain my health and make wellness a priority.

This is yet another place where we can mistakenly pretend to have two lives. We put wellness in the personal category as if it is a luxury that we will pay attention to when things calm down at work. The reality is, the busier we are professionally, the more seriously we need to focus on our wellness if we want to achieve our unique potential and the success that comes with it. Like a broken record, I will say it again: neither your unique potential nor your success has to be defined by career milestones any more than it has to be defined by personal milestones. Your unique potential and your success are merely an expression of achieving the most out of your one life, as *you* define it.

Getting healthy was a critical part of my *business* plan. I slowly began to eat better and even more slowly regained an active lifestyle. The final piece of the puzzle came when I met my life partner, and best friend who happens to be my wife, Deb. She taught me more about what good food and the critical importance of SLEEP are in three months than I had learned in my entire life. Today my physician proclaims that my blood work and my body are more like those of a thirty-year-old amateur athlete than those of a considerably older small-business owner. My mind has never been sharper; my energy levels have never been higher; and my cardio threshold is very close to what it was thirty years ago.

So this is why I believe that, even though I'm not credentialed, I'm not a doctor, and I have no formal training in fitness or nutrition (outside of an expired personal trainer certification), I have something to offer the average adult who wants to achieve a high level of wellness. Best of all, none of this is hard; you just have to apply the three *P*s. In this case, the purpose is a high level of wellness.

Initially what will drive the passion and provide that fuel is going to be a vision of a happier, healthier, more vivacious, and more self-confident person with a better self-image and a better outlook. You have to be able to see this and feel this vision, because initially it will be just that, a vision. Changing your health through better living is a relatively slow process, so you must hang on to that vision of the new you. Passion is critical to success, because without that fuel you will not be able to maintain the persistence required to get to your purpose. I assure you that once you start feeling better, once you start sleeping better, once you experience how much clearer you are thinking and how much less annoyed and frustrated you are, that passion will flow like never before.

Nutrition basics:

- Drink more water, about .6 ounces per day per pound of body weight.
- Eat everything *slowly*
- NEVER diet; change the way you eat forever.

- NEVER, smoke or chew tobacco
- Eat less more frequently—five or six times a day about two hours apart.
- Sleep at least seven hours; eight is ideal for most. This is second only to water in importance.
- Eliminate processed food; eat things as close to their natural state as possible.
- Eat no trans fats and minimize saturated fat.
- Minimize sugar; go for less than 30 grams of processed sugar a day.

There you have them: the critical fundamental basics of nutrition. Notice there is nothing on eliminating fat or carbs or whatever. Much of what you know and what you have been told and taught about nutrition is not accurate. Even the information that is accurate is presented in such a complicated way that you either believe it on faith or give up trying to understand it. People are so desperate to lose weight (not necessarily to live healthier) and at least temporarily to look better, they will try almost anything. Mix this primal desire to be thinner with a free-market society, and you have thousands of people offering you the quick fix, the simple solution, the meal in a box, or the secret shake meal replacement.

The truth is, you want to lose body fat—I will use the term *body fat* and *inches*—not lose weight going forward, because weight is a highly inaccurate measurement of progress when seeking a higher level of wellness. The simple truth is, if you seek to lose fat and inches off your body, you must consume fewer calories than you burn. To lose a pound of fat, you must have a caloric deficit of about 3,500 calories. So if you want to lose two pounds a week of actual body fat, you need to burn 7,000 calories more than you consume. Diets claiming a weight loss of five, six, or more pounds in a week need to be looked at with extreme caution.

Fat loss programs come and go, but can you quickly name the program that has been around essentially unchanged since 1963? Over fifty years and counting—thousands of other programs have come and gone, but Weight Watchers marches on. Although I do not agree with all the foods you are allowed to eat on the Weight Watchers program, I absolutely agree with the approach: eat fewer calories than you burn, and you will lose fat. Weight Watchers has made it a little simpler with a points system, since nobody likes to count calories, but essentially that is what you're doing with your points. Not all calories are created equal, and Weight Watchers steers you to better choices by assigning higher point values to less desirable or higher-saturated-fat foods.

The first question is, how many calories do you burn right now? I recommend the website www.everydayhealth.com, where you can find out your base metabolic rate (BMR), based on your age, gender, and activity level. Your base metabolic rate is how many calories you burn in a twenty-four-hour period. Here are some interesting numbers for you: for a forty-year-old woman who is five foot five, weighs 135 pounds, and is sedentary—outside of walking to the car or walking to the office or light walking around the store, she does not move much—the base metabolic rate is 1,600 calories.

When we talk about exercise, we will learn that if this woman starts an exercise program where she becomes moderately active, her base metabolic rate will go up 350 calories a day to 1,950. For a fifty-year-old man who is six feet tall and weighs 180 pounds, the base metabolic rate is 2,100 calories. If he were to become moderately active, his base metabolic rate would increase to 2,500 calories. Moderately active is thirty to forty-five minutes of movement that elevates your heart rate, four days a week. I will say more about this when I talk about exercise, so just look at the numbers now. If a moderately active woman at the age of forty was trying to lose two pounds of body fat per week, she has already lost three-quarters of a pound of fat without doing anything to her diet. The man described above would lose a full pound of fat.

Here is where the bad math comes into play. If I really want to lose a lot of weight, I'll just eat 700 or 800 calories a day. If my base metabolic rate is 1,700 calories, I will be able to lose two pounds of fat per week without having to do anything differently. Unfortunately, the human body does whatever it needs to survive. If you are only consuming 700 or 800 calories a day, you are starving your body. When your body feels that it is being starved, it begins to conserve energy in any way possible.

So, what might have been a 1,700-calorie BMR without activity becomes a 1,400 or 1,300 BMR when you start to starve your body. That's why some of these so-called rapid weight-loss diets are so frightening. They combine a severely restricted diet with amphetamines. And people on these extreme weight loss diets are told not to exercise. That's because these diets dangerous; the body is already under extreme stress. Physical activity could be catastrophic. As I have said numerous times, I am not a doctor; I am simply a person who has read and lived and read and lived. Super restricted-calorie diets are dangerous.

Here's another one that comes into play often when I'm talking to people about eating better. They tell me it is either too expensive to eat well or too time consuming. Many of these people drop thirty or forty dollars a week on some crazy, dangerous diet pill. Or they spend seventy-five or a hundred dollars or more a month on food that comes in cardboard boxes delivered to their mailbox. Yummy.

Again, the most important and most beneficial supplement you can put in your body is good, clean water. Never, smoke or chew tobacco and sleep at least 7 hours every day and off you go. We have trademarked a logo for our wellness brand, and it is no accident that a water droplet is prominent.

Well BEING

One Life™

If you don't have one already, get yourself a BPA-free plastic water bottle that holds at least twenty-four ounces of water. Keep it full and sip water all day long. I could fill up more space with what BPAs are, but just trust me that they are not good for the body and are found in cheap plastic drinking containers and most aluminum canned goods.

Let me digress a little bit on the multigazillion-dollar bottled water business. For the most part, this is great marketing and not much more. The majority of tap water in the United States is monitored and tested to make sure it is safe for cooking and drinking. That being said, some of it tastes kind of funny, and I've never fully believed I can count on a city, state, or federal commission or agency to make sure what goes in my body is safe. I therefore double filter the tap water I drink. I have a filter on the water in my refrigerator, and that water goes through a second filter in my water pitcher.

I'm hopeful I get thousands and thousands of e-mails telling me what bad advice this is and how dangerous tap water is. Mostly I'm hoping to get thousands and thousands of e-mails because that would mean quite a few people actually read this book, which is my intention, because I believe it can help people fundamentally change all aspects of their life. That aside, I take double filtration of a known, tested, municipal water source and save the tens of millions of bottles of plastic that are going to landfills. So, fill that BPA-free water bottle with tap water that has been single or double filtered, and drink it all day long.

Back on point. Eating better does not cost more. In fact, if you eat fresh fruit, fresh vegetables, and organic poultry, meats, and fish, you will not throw away 30 to 40 percent of your food, which is the average that Americans throw away. If you have ever spent a significant amount of time in Europe, you know how most Europeans shop for food: they buy for the day or for two days at most. If you eat food close to when it was on a bush or tree, in the ground, or swimming, flying, or running, you will be eating fresh food. So instead of that trek to the grocery store every other week to drop who knows how much money, stop by on your way home from work and buy enough for tonight and tomorrow.

If you have kids in the house, this is not going to work, because kids love snacks. If you have lousy, sugar- and chemical-loaded snacks with more preservatives than actual food in them, that is what they will eat. If you have a nice selection of nutrition bars, some fruit, and some nuts, they will get eaten. "You don't know my kids"—yup, I can hear you saying it; fill in *partner, spouse,* etc., for kids and I still hear you. Worst-case scenario is the garbage is out of your house, replaced by good, real food, and if they don't eat it, they will lose some weight and you have more healthy snacks for you. Wow, no downside! Buy bulk organic chicken, organic beef, or organic hamburger. Want some great snacks to take with you during the week? On Sunday evening, cook or grill two organic chicken breasts. Slice them in finger-size pieces, and take four or five in a Ziploc bag in a little portable cooler with you to work each day. You'll get an amazing source of protein with little fat and no carbohydrates. So, it is a myth that eating healthy food costs more money than eating garbage.

Eating out is an entirely different matter. I have a little restaurant guide app on my iPhone and my iPad. While traveling, this little puppy comes in handy. It allows me to look at the nutritional content of the food in the majority of chain and fast-food restaurants. You might look up a fast-food restaurant and see that KFC offers fried chicken loaded with saturated fat and calories, and this is certainly a choice. What you may not pay attention to is the picnic-size pinto beans. This may not be a meal, but it is certainly a better choice than the fried chicken. With less than four hundred calories, it has twenty-three grams of protein, nineteen grams of fiber, seventy grams of complex carbohydrates, and only one gram of fat. Yes, it has a great deal of sodium, and sodium is not your friend, but given the choice between the chicken and the beans, go with the beans. It's probably not enough for a meal for a man, but it is for most women. Don't get a soda. Just get water, and you will have a substantial snack or a meal that is of fairly high quality and will cost less than three dollars.

Stopping for breakfast? You could do worse than the McDonald's Egg McMuffin. Although it does contain twelve grams of fat, it has three hundred calories and eighteen grams of protein. Again, I'm not advocating eating at any restaurant regularly; it is simply too risky because you really don't know what's in the food. But at any chain restaurant you can find reasonably healthy alternatives. It's going to be tough to do without checking out the posted nutritional guides in many of these restaurants or without some type of book or app, since many of the things we think are healthy are anything but.

It's time now for my list of favorite foods. These are not necessarily the foods I enjoy the most; they are the ones I eat most frequently to maintain my weight and muscle mass.

- Legumes, beans. I love black beans, pinto beans, navy beans, and lima beans. Remember, a can of baked beans loaded with sugar does not meet the criteria we discussed earlier. Boiling your own is best, but flash frozen is OK too.
- Peanut butter. My go-to snack of choice is natural peanut butter. No need to go to a health food store—most major brands now have a natural peanut butter. As is the case with all sorts of food, just because it says "natural" on the label does not mean it's good for you. It may have palm oil or sugar added, since both technically are natural. I eat a brand that has one ingredient: peanuts.
- Speaking of nuts, almonds are another favorite food of mine. Avoid salted or smoked varieties, as they have a ton of sodium. (sea salt is better than regular salt)
- Vegetables of all kinds—the more colorful the better. I will freely admit I don't like vegetables. I do not like them at all. But I always try to eat vegetables anyway.
- Fish, grilled or baked—in fact, pretty much any seafood. Yes, I know shellfish is often high in cholesterol, but it is also low in fat and high in protein. With respect to cholesterol, if you ate nothing but shrimp, it would raise the bad cholesterol, LDL. But several studies have indicated it increases the good cholesterol, HDL, by an offsetting amount.
- Oatmeal. Steel-cut oats are wonderful but take a long time to cook, so I just used unflavored instant oatmeal. Again, for all the reasons already discussed, avoid flavored oatmeal, which is loaded with sugar and who knows what else.
- Eggs. Yes, eggs are often considered evil because of their cholesterol and fat content, but an egg is protein in its best form. You can ditch the yolks; egg whites are pure protein.

- Lean cuts of beef, poultry. You need protein, and although there are ways to get protein from things such as nuts, eggs, or protein supplements, beef and poultry—especially organic beef and poultry—are a wonderful source of protein.
- Whole-grain bread. I'm Portuguese, and to tell a Portuguese person not to eat bread is the equivalent of telling him not to breathe. That being said, eat whole-grain breads. If the first ingredient includes the word *enriched*, it is not whole grain. I'm a particular fan of darker breads, such as rye or a form of rye, pumpernickel.
- Berries. I love strawberries, raspberries, blueberries. These are wonderful foods. If they're not in season and you can get them flash frozen, please do. They are full of antioxidants and tasty. They really make you feel that you're eating something bad when you aren't.

I'd like to finish this section on nutrition with what I call the guilty-pleasure clause. Once a week, typically on a Friday night or Saturday or Sunday, I eat garbage, like three pieces of pepperoni pizza or a cheeseburger and fries. Food that clearly is not something you want to make a steady diet out of. I don't give it a second thought, and it doesn't affect my body fat, my cholesterol, or any other aspect of my health. I eat four to six times a day, so if once a week I eat junk but I eat well the other thirty-five to forty-two times, my one junk meal has no effect. The exception to this rule is if you are trying to lose weight. Throwing away seven hundred or eight hundred calories on a guilty-pleasure meal might make an aggressive fat loss plan of two pounds per week difficult to achieve. In this case, try one small piece of pepperoni pizza or half a cheeseburger.

Forget Exercise, Move with Purpose

We are always getting ready to live but never living.
–Ralph Waldo Emerson

Just as you replace the word *diet* with the thought of eating better, replace the word *exercise* with the thought of moving more often. We need to do more than move, though; we also need to do resistance training—that is, exercise that challenges your muscles. We start to lose muscle mass at about age forty. And we lose between 2 and 2½ percent of our muscle mass each year. So, yes, that means by the time you're fifty, you have lost 20 to 25 percent of your muscle mass—unless you do something about it.

Not only is it possible to stop the loss, but you can actually add muscle mass. Earlier I wrote about being thirty pounds heavier than I was in the early 1980s, although my waist has gone only from size 30 to 32 due to adding muscle mass. The better news if you're past forty is most of these gains in my mass occurred after I turned forty. My approach to nutrition and moving with purpose produces real results that last for years.

I have helped dozens of people either regain a level of fitness or maintain a level of fitness. It is not impossible; you just have to be committed to it.

Once again the three *P*s come into play: passion, persistence, and purpose. I will not pretend to be an expert in all things fitness and nutrition, but I certainly have learned enough by trial and error and relentless research, observation, and self-experimentation to know more than the majority of laypeople. To sum it up, you could do a lot worse than to be in the physical condition I am in, even if you're twenty-five years younger than I am. So please read on.

For those that want to achieve their unique potential and realize their upside, wellness is a necessity. So in keeping with that theme, stop thinking in terms of exercise and start thinking in terms of moving with purpose. The word *diet* does not typically evoke positive emotions in people. The word *exercise* has a similar effect, though likely it's not quite as negative. Nonetheless, we're talking about fundamentally changing the way we live, and that is not done via exercise; it is done by moving with purpose.

When we fully understand the concept of moving with purpose, we park on the far side of the parking lot at the grocery store or at work. We cut lunchtime in half and walk briskly for half of it. When we take the stairs instead of the elevator up two flights, we're moving with purpose. If you have a sturdy coffee table or hard-seated chair and enough room to stretch out on the floor, you have a gym. I do not travel as much as I used to, but travel is no excuse not to move with purpose. Your body is your gym. Add a simple resistance band (rubber hoses with handles), and you have an advanced home or travel gym. Your only important investment is a good-quality pair of cross-training sneakers.

My desire here is just to get you in the mind-set to achieve wellness. Moving with purpose is cumulative. For example, four ten-minute walks throughout the day will get your heart rate up into a fat-burning zone that's equivalent to forty straight minutes of cardio workout. So the excuse "I don't have time" is exactly that—an excuse. "I cannot afford a gym membership" or "I do not have time to get to the gym" are other excuses, because you do not need a gym membership and you do not need to get to a gym. "I cannot afford" or "I do not have room" for a treadmill, elliptical, recumbent bicycle, weight bench, free weights, or whatever. Again, none of that is required. Simple resistance bands that you can buy for fifteen to twenty-five dollars (get one with a "door attachment") plus a chair, a coffee table, a wall, and free space where you can lie down is your gymnasium.

Aging is required; growing old is optional. Read Deepak Chopra's *Grow Younger, Live Longer*, a fascinating book that destroys the myth that our bodies are locked into "calendar-based" deterioration. There are people in their sixties, seventies, and even eighties and beyond that walk and stretch and move with purpose every day. My dad walked down the hill and got his paper every morning till he was about ninety. There are people stricken with disease, physical ailments, or handicaps that restrict varying degrees of movement who stay fit. Look no further than the power of the Special Olympics. *The next time Special Olympics trials are held in near you, go watch them, and then tell yourself what you can't do.*

For a great resistance band and whole-body cardio and resistance training workout, check out *10 Minute Trainer* from the folks at www. beachbody.com. It is a workout led by Tony Horton from P90X workout fame. It's pretty intense, but not nearly as intense as P90X; it uses your body and resistance bands extensively. I'm not saying there are no other programs out there; I encourage you to find a program. Making up your own can be unproductive and even dangerous.

Here is something you may not want to read, but I encourage you to read it anyway and to take it to heart. When achieving your unique potential, you are likely to have a huge obstacle to overcome. That huge obstacle is *you*. More than any other factor, regardless of how severe that factor is (short of death), you are your biggest obstacle to eating better and moving with purpose. We love to blame life, they, them, the in-laws, the children, this house, the boss, the parents, the neighbor, the weather, the city, the government, and so on, but the major obstacle for you not moving with purpose, for you not achieving more, for not being happier, for not being where you dream of being, is you. You are your own worst enemy. The great news is, you are also absolutely your most powerful resource.

I wrote about this earlier in the book, but it is too powerful not to write about again. According to an article in the *Archives of Internal Medicine,* the leading causes of type 2 diabetes in adults are lack of physical activity, body fat (obesity), poor eating habits (bad nutritional intake), smoking (using any type of tobacco product), and excessive alcohol use. If we look at this list, we can see that we have control over every one of these factors. In fact, the article goes on to say that 90 percent of type II diabetes in this country is preventable—*90 percent*. How about this one: according to the Mayo Clinic, *80 percent of heart disease is preventable*. So if there are two hundred people suffering from either heart disease, the leading killer of Americans, or the debilitating disease of type II diabetes, 170 of those two hundred have at least partially contributed to their disease.

It's more amazing that thirty to forty minutes of elevated heart-rate movement, combined with ten or fifteen minutes of resistance training three or four times a week in conjunction with a reasonable nutritional plan along the lines of what I suggest, is all that's needed to dramatically reduce your odds of suffering from heart disease or diabetes. This assumes you use absolutely no tobacco products and you consume alcohol only in moderation, and that you sleep at least 7 hours per night. Move with purpose and eat healthier, and you can live a significantly happier and healthier life.

Life does not come with guarantees; any of us can be struck down by an accident or illness at any time. But why on earth would you not take the simple, easy steps to reduce the risk in areas you do control? Keep in mind, please, that heart disease is the number-one killer of Americans. I know I've said this before, but why would you not take the simple steps not to become part of that statistic? Remember, 90 percent of type II diabetes is preventable with the simple methods we talk about in these two wellness chapters. Nearly twenty-six million Americans—over 8 percent of our adult population—suffer from type II diabetes. Upward of twenty-three million people could avoid diabetes with little more than the advice provided in the nutrition and move-with-purpose chapters. Why would anyone expose himself to the horrors of diabetes and heart disease when the majority of it is so easy to prevent? And remember, the factors that lead to type II diabetes are the same factors that contribute most significantly to heart disease. 'Nuff said.

Don't Let People Live Rent Free in Your Head

An ounce of action is worth a ton of theory.
—Ralph Waldo Emerson

The first time I heard, "Don't let people live rent free in your head" was at one of the first Alcoholics Anonymous meetings I attended. Back in the very beginning of my journey to sobriety, it seemed that every meeting was filled with phrases, with short little nuggets. Things like "one day at a time," "live the serenity prayer," "drop the rock," and the title of this chapter. It's not really the purpose of this book to talk about how I got sober, but it seems important to this chapter to go a little further than simply saying I did.

I can distinctly remember the smell of the meeting room: burnt coffee and cigarettes. Coffee and cigarettes are the staple at most every AA meeting, although now most smoking is outside the door, but the black coffee is still the same. Having spent twenty years in the navy, I was extremely familiar with both coffee and cigarettes, so that was one of the few things that I felt comfortable with being in those meetings. I can remember looking around the rooms, listening to the stories, kind of going through the motions and telling myself over and over, "I don't belong here."

Another phrase that I heard often, "fake it until you make it," was something I was doing, and I had no idea if I was going to make it. The majority of people that are successful using the twelve-step program at Alcoholics Anonymous get a sponsor—a mentor or coach—early on. Even though I was brand new, I figured I didn't need to do what everybody else did, so I could do without a sponsor. So I would sit in meeting after meeting and listen to story after story and phrase after phrase, and I would dismiss them almost as fast as I heard them.

But one kept ringing in the back of my mind. "Don't let people live rent free in your head." The more I thought about this one, the more it rang true with how I had lived. When I got upset, when I got angry when somebody said something to me that I thought was improper or hurtful, it ate at me for days, weeks, or even months. After a while, it would either fade or turn into full-blown resentment. Or I would find an opportunity to explode with a verbal barrage. Often that barrage was not toward the person who had been living rent free in my head. Instead I decapitated an innocent bystander with words.

In the military, we would call this collateral damage. Yep, I caused a considerable amount of collateral damage. Pondering this phrase led me to a question: how much of my life had been spent obsessing, stressing, and eating myself up over someone who likely remembered nothing about what I was choking on? The answer: more than I could imagine and more than I wanted to spend going forward. The easy part was understanding this; it would not prove so easy to do something about it.

As with everything else I've achieved, step one was figuring out what the outcome was. In this case, the outcome was simple: stop letting people live rent free in my head. Or in even simpler terms: stop obsessing about things people say or do. Next up was putting together the action plan. And I missed the mark by completely oversimplifying things. I decided that I would allow people to "bother me" for twenty-four hours, and then I would let it go. (I'll take a break from writing now so you can have a good chuckle.)

Our brain is an amazing thing, and it doesn't understand the word *don't*. For example, I am going to write something here, and I want you to read it very quickly:

Don't think about a purple elephant doing somersaults in your front yard.

Was the first thing that flashed through your mind anything other than a purple elephant doing somersaults? So when we say the word *don't*, anything that follows is the first thing the mind thinks about. So when we correct children starting with the word *don't*, we often reinforce the behavior we don't want to see again. Once you understand that basic reaction, you realize you have to work past it to blank out the word.

Here's how it works: Your mind processes "let people live rent free in your head." *Huh?* is what happens next. Why would I want people to live rent free in my head, what does that even mean? So because of the wording, we confuse our minds and it forces us to process further. So now the word *don't* gets applied, and it absolutely makes your mind "deal" with that statement.

So when I missed this powerful point and told myself "don't think" about whatever the cause was or whatever the person did, after twenty-four hours I had little chance of success. In fact, I did not succeed. What turned out to be very powerful for me was this: if you want to see change in others, you must first change yourself. So rather than trying to do the impossible and shutting my brain down from thinking about what another person did, I had to change my action or my reaction to produce a different outcome. I had to speak with the other person about what was bothering me. Whether they agreed, accepted my statement, or my requests did not change the fact that as soon as I finished the conversation they were no longer in my head.

Almost immediately I discovered two critical things that I think you can benefit from. First, when I forced myself to act, that person was removed from my thoughts, because I simply confronted him or her directly, politely, and immediately. Second, I would always imagine how horrible the conversation was going to be, how unreceptive the other person was going to be, and how much of a battle the conversation would be. But that was almost never the case. When you delay having a tough conversation with someone for days, weeks, or months, you often find out it was much simpler, much less painful, and much easier than you thought it would be. In fact, you regret putting it off for so long. This is how you stop letting people live rent free in your head. Take action, the same theme continues.

When I was a command master chief of a training command, I had a magnificent administrative assistant who essentially ran the day-to-day operations of my job. She was bright, articulate, and fierce, and I have great respect for her. One day I was walking down the main road of the base and saw her on the other side of the street, walking in the opposite direction. I'd loudly called out her name and said a loud hello. She looked directly at me but did not acknowledge me in any way.

Over the next week, she lived rent free in my head. The more I thought about how she ignored me, the more upset I got. My tone changed around her; my demeanor changed around her; and the entire nature of our relationship changed. This was not my impression, but hers. How do I know this? After about a week, she approached me and asked what was going on. Of course I said, "Nothing." She pointed out all the changes in my behavior toward her and went on to say that she felt I was somehow annoyed, disappointed, or otherwise upset with her.

This midlevel petty officer, whom I had spent many hours coaching, mentoring, and developing, was now teaching me. The student had become the master. I came clean and told her about the incident. I told her how I felt disrespected and how I did not understand how two people that had such a great rapport could have something like this occur. I was prepared for an intelligent explanation of why she had chosen to ignore me that day. I expected this because she always had a well-thought-out reason for everything she did.

Such was not the case this day. She simply looked at me and said, "Master Chief, I have no idea what you're talking about." She hadn't heard me or seen me on the road; it was just a coincidence that she'd looked in my direction. So actually there was not even an event, except in my mind; my reaction had led me to let her "rude behavior" bounce around in my head.

I will be so bold as to say you have done this; very few people haven't. It is unhealthy and unwise. I encourage you to take a break from your reading and think about this as it applies to your own life. Think about the last time you let somebody linger in your mind for days or weeks. What could that time have been used for?

If I were more analytical, if I were more of a thinker, it's likely I wouldn't have given two seconds of thought to what occurred that day. But if you are a thinker, if you are an analytical person that is not overly emotional and does not spend much time with feelings, you are fooling yourself if you believe there are no instances when people say hurtful things and you wind up spending hours or days or longer replaying the conversation. In fact, a thinker or analytical person will dissect the conversation or the incident a thousand different ways, whereas a feeler just feels bad. The thinker has to drill down and figure out the root cause, what was said, what actions occurred, and so on. The point is, whether you're approaching this from a feelings point of view or from a thinking, analytical, logical point of view, when someone gets inside your head, you lose time that you will never get back. *Don't let people live rent free in your head.*

At the root of letting people live rent free in your head are two things: assumptions and taking things personally. It's very hard not to take things personally, especially if you are a feelings person. It is even harder not to make assumptions and to force yourself to react based only on what you know to be the facts. Trying to operate from "what you know" (facts) versus what you think or feel (almost always loaded with assumption) is very difficult to do. You must constantly ask yourself, "Is this something I know or something I think/feel?" Do this *continuously* and do this *before* you react and eventually your unconscious *will begin to reprogram* itself to a more fact based unconscious.

The Four Agreements, by Don Miguel Ruiz, is a great little book on these two topics, plus two other topics of extreme importance in leading a healthier life emotionally and spiritually. It really nails it. The Four Agreements are:

- Always do your best.
- Make no assumptions.
- Take nothing personally.
- Be impeccable with your word.

The book goes into great detail about the origins of these four agreements as well as the agreements themselves and how they can and will benefit you. My attempts in recent years to live by these agreements has changed my life, who I am, and my relationships with others. Very powerful stuff. It also is a great lead-in to the last chapter of this book.

The Spiritual Side

Unless you try to do something beyond what you have already mastered, you will never grow.
—Ralph Waldo Emerson

Our Father, who art in heaven, hallowed be thy name. Thy kingdom come, thy will be done on earth as it is in heaven. Give us this day our daily bread and forgive us our trespasses as we forgive those who trespass against us. Lead us not into temptation, but deliver us from evil.

As a kid, this was part of my prayers before bedtime and something I heard every Sunday morning in church. There were many years I stopped doing any praying and never wanted to go to church, although I did. I was surprised to hear it at the end of the first AA meeting I attended.

I heard that prayer and the Serenity Prayer:

God, grant me the serenity to accept the things I cannot change, the courage to change the things I can, and the wisdom to know the difference.

These two prayers became the foundation of my first true spiritual journey. I debated about writing on spirituality in this book. On the one hand, I firmly believe that without some type of spiritual base it is impossible to achieve you unique potential in life. Along with emotional, physical, and mental development, it forms our foundation; it makes us grounded so that we can build. So it is critical to the theme of this book. On the other hand, who the heck am I to offer advice in an area that I have discovered only recently? Without question, this little chapter would never have been written without the insistence of my life partner, Deb.

I'm not going to offer advice here; I'm going to share my story. Perhaps it will strike a chord—maybe a negative chord—but it is my story and I've never been one to shy away from a bit of risk. So here goes—starting first at the end, today.

I have grown to respect all religious beliefs, all spiritual beliefs, for not to do so puts me in a position to judge what is most sacred to so many people throughout the world. If what you believe does not harm others, believe away! My partner's mother said something to me one day that struck me smack between the eyes: "I don't understand people when they say I've got to go to church; I *get* to go to church." Wow, that is a great one! I end every evening with prayer and start every day with prayer, and God is with me in everything I do. But it was not always so and I am in no way, shape or form steering you towards any belief. After all believing in nothing external to you, is absolutely believing in something. I encourage you to be open to something more, but at the end of the day go with whatever works for you.

I was raised Roman Catholic. My Sunday mornings were spent in church. Everybody dressed in his or her Sunday best. In church there were lots of robes, lots of candles; it was all very serious, very stoic. I freely admit leaving church most Sundays feeling worse about myself than when I entered. It felt like four parts guilt and one part "you need to do better." I was a little guy, but I really can remember thinking, "Isn't the point of all this to leave feeling better than you did when you came in, not worse?"

Without question, I never wanted to go to church; I was made to go to church, and at some point either my parents gave up on making me go or I got old enough that I didn't have to go. But I do remember not missing it. Over the next twenty-five years, I went to church to support my wife at the time. She thought it was important to raise our two children with a religious foundation. Frankly, I did not really agree with that, since I never got anything out of it, but I did attend church with her and our children, participated and encouraged them to do the same.

I cannot remember a single time when I genuinely prayed in all those years. I was completely void of spirituality in any form, and I'm pretty sure it showed. It wasn't until I committed to sobriety in November of 2002 that I finally reconnected with the spiritual side of me. Alcoholics Anonymous reintroduced me to the concept of a higher power and led me to a strong belief in something much greater than myself, something, or more correctly, *someone*, I came to call God. Chapter 5 of the book *Alcoholics Anonymous*, "How It Works," contains the twelve steps. I am going to share these steps with you and then tell you how they lead me to God.

1. We admitted we were powerless over alcohol, that our lives had become unmanageable;
2. Came to believe that a power greater than ourselves could restore us to sanity;
3. Made a decision to turn our will and our lives over to the care of God as we understood him;
4. Made a searching and fearless moral inventory of ourselves;
5. Admitted to God, to ourselves, and to another human being the exact nature of our wrongs;
6. Were entirely ready to have God remove all these defects of character;
7. Humbly asked him to remove our shortcomings;

8. Made a list of all persons we had harmed, and became willing to make amends to them all;

9. Made direct amends to such people wherever possible, except when to do so would injure them or others;

10. Continued to take personal inventory and when we were wrong promptly admitted it;

11. Sought through prayer and meditation to improve our conscious contact with God as we understood him, praying only for knowledge of his will for us and the power to carry that out;

12. Having had a spiritual awakening as the result of these steps, we tried to carry this message to alcoholics, and to practice these principles in all our affairs.

Everybody's journey to sobriety is unique. So in that respect, this chapter fits the theme of achieving your unique potential. It also fits because if you struggle with some form of addiction and feel a need to connect to some being, something greater than yourself I would say, why not try this? Others might simply be curious to read my personal journey to enlightenment. If you are none of the above, there's another chapter that will speak to you—this I promise. But before dismissing this chapter, hang in there just a bit longer.

As I stated in the chapter on nutrition, there's a reason Weight Watchers has been around so long; it's one of the few programs that is not only based on science but also based on common sense. It has had longevity because it works. The book *Alcoholics Anonymous* was written in 1939. The twelve steps have longevity because they work.

In my early sobriety, I was extremely mechanical in my approach. The steps were a checklist for me. I clearly had gotten to a point that I could not control my drinking; things were getting worse; and it was getting harder and harder to live the lie. Check step one.

For about a year previously, I had tried all sorts of different things to control the insanity of my drinking, but nothing worked. Out of desperation, having tried everything else I could, I thought maybe, just maybe, there is some greater power out there that could help me. Step two and three took nearly ten years. Yes, it took me that long to turn my will over to the care of God. Initially I faked it, then I slowly opened up to the idea, and finally I really let go.

I checked off four, five, and six over numerous months of early sobriety. I discovered prayer, real prayer. This was not prayer to ask God to get me out of trouble or to cover up lies that still came out of my mouth with great regularity. It was real prayer, simply asking God to remove this demon called alcoholism from my soul. Check to step seven.

I worked through steps eight, nine, and ten, though frankly not as thoroughly as I should have. These steps occurred at a time that I felt fairly solid in my sobriety, and I did not devote as much time as I should have. Regret is one of the biggest enemies of sobriety, so I have forgiven myself for not fully committing to those three steps. I have since gone back and have tried to do better.

Step eleven has been at my side since I drew my first sober breath in 2002. Although it is listed above, I'm going to repeat it here: *Sought through prayer and meditation to improve our conscious contact with God as we understood him, praying only for knowledge of his will for us and the power to carry that out.* There is much pain, suffering, and agony in the first ten steps—not just for the person seeking sobriety but also for those close to her or him. Steps eleven and twelve are the maintenance steps. I struggled with honesty, transparency, and openness for years, after getting sober. I never stopped praying for knowledge of his will and the power to carry it out.

As I said earlier, it took years for me to turn my will over to the care of God, just as it took years for me to simply pray to God for knowledge of his will and the power to carry it out, and nothing more. For years I was faking it, hoping someday to make it.

I have bared my soul in about every area in writing to strangers all over the world. I have only stayed away from one specific area. You will find no reference to my spiritual or religious beliefs other than I have a belief in a higher power that I choose to call God. As my relationship with God has grown, it has helped me in every possible way. I remain a grateful recovering alcoholic. I believe I can continue on this path with God's help. I have found the miracle of honesty and transparency. The energy and stress that comes with trying to juggle lies and secrets tears every fiber of your soul. I believe that a life void of spirituality, however you choose to see it, is a life half lived. My relationship with God is as necessary for my survival as water and food and sleep. In fact, God nurtures me in a way neither food nor water, nor sleep can.

It has only been a very short amount of time since I found a place to gather with others, and feel completely and totally comfortable in, to worship, meditate, pray, fill in the blank _____ as I see fit. As is the case with many other areas of my life, my partner is responsible for introducing me to this place. On a typical Sunday, there is almost always a point when I get choked up, and often my eyes well up with tears over something profound I hear or I see. I also have never made it through a service without a belly laugh—and I've never felt it was inappropriate.

I am surrounded by love and I am cradled in God's arms, and that feeling is never stronger than when I spend time with that crazy cast of characters on Sunday morning. I know that only a few years ago I would have not been able to "get it" that God is great. When I leave those services, I have energy radiating from inside me. It is unmatched by any energy I have ever felt. It far surpasses the exhilaration of a hike in the mountains, a swim in the ocean, stargazing, or mountain biking on a tough, tranquil, and desolate trail. Now *that* is saying something.

It has energized me to have more meaningful prayer and to have more powerful periods of meditation in my daily life. I don't worry as I used to—and I used to worry about everything. My mental disorder makes it easy for me to be anxious almost to the point of not functioning, yet I barely feel any anxiety anymore. Prayer, for me, is a key ingredient in my calmer mental state.

If you know exactly how I feel, I hope you share this with friends and family that perhaps are either searching or just simply don't believe. Spirituality is a profoundly personal thing, so I would never advocate lecturing or forcing anyone to do anything they are not freely willing to do. If you have found meditation to be profoundly helpful to you, reach out and invite someone you care about to join you. If you've found, as Deb and I have, a wonderful place to share spirituality, invite someone that you think might benefit to come along one day.

This book is not about converting, transforming, or making anybody believe what I believe; we are, after all, unique. As has been said with respect to communication, accountability, nutrition, seeking out your talent, and every other thought in this book, there is something for everyone. This chapter on spirituality is not the exception.

I started this chapter with a prayer I learned in a Roman Catholic church. But it really had meaning for me for the first time in a shadowy room above an old furniture store when I started to attend AA meetings in Pensacola, Florida. I will end with the second prayer—the Serenity Prayer—I hope it touches you as it has me for all these years.

God, grant me the serenity to accept the things I cannot change, the courage to change the things I can, and the wisdom to know the difference.

About the Author

Would you like to have John Gregory speak at an upcoming event, or perhaps you are seeking personal coaching? Contact him directly at jgv@gconsultinggrp.com

John Gregory Vincent was born in Greenlawn, New York, more than a few years ago. Shy and withdrawn for most of his first eighteen years, he was an average student with close friends, but few friends. It was when he attended college at the State University at New York Maritime College in the Bronx, New York, that he really felt his bond with the sea and came out of his self-created shell. After getting tossed from college, he did what many young men and a few women did back in the day: he enlisted in the military. It was years later that he figured out his navy recruiter's true purpose when he suggested John go into submarines (recruiters got bonuses for getting volunteers for submarine service back then), but John remembers clearly the thought of, "How do you navigate underneath the ocean?" had him hooked instantly. The navy was quite literally a lifesaver for a young man completely out of control, making daily dangerous and reckless decisions that almost certainly would have resulted in injury, jail, or worse.

He married fairly young and was married for twenty-five years. Pretty good years early on, not so good as time went on, it nonetheless was a major portion of his life and really helped push him toward the needed, sweeping changes he has made in more recent years in all aspects of his one life.

Retiring from the navy after twenty years, most of which were spent on operational submarines, he went on to work in the broadcast television advertising world for several years, enjoying great success initially as a salesperson and then as a sales manager. He resigned in 2008 and started the Genesis Group LLC, a thriving, growing, human capital firm, specializing in management development.

A grateful recovering alcoholic, he returned to school nearly twenty years after being tossed out, finished his undergraduate degree, and went on to obtain his MBA. At the time of the writing of this revision of the book, he lives in Bostic NC, with his life partner, best friend and wife, Deb, and their four, four-legged children (two dogs, two cats). John will tell you life doesn't begin at any specific age. It begins when you take charge of it. He hopes you do just that and that this book enhances your journey.

www.ingramcontent.com/pod-product-compliance
Lightning Source LLC
LaVergne TN
LVHW021454080426
835509LV00018B/2276